KILTS, CONFETTI & CONSPIRACY

By

Bill Shackleton

Published by
Cauliay Publishing & Distribution
PO Box 12076
Aberdeen
AB16 9AL
www.cauliaypublishing.com

First Edition
ISBN 978-0-9554964-7-9
Copyright © Bill Shackleton 2008

Front cover picture.
Cover design. © Cauliay Publishing

A CIP catalogue record for this book is available from the British Library.

For

Margaret, Alison, Joy
Gillian and wee Gracie

INTRODUCTION

Permit me a batch of clichés in this introduction to Bill Shackleton's latest opus. Here is the first. The Scots are not noted for their humour. As the immortal Wodehouse pointed out many years ago it is not difficult to tell the difference between a ray of sunshine and a Scot with a grievance. When the word "Scot" comes up in the media it is invariably preceded with the word "dour". This is because when a Scot is in England he has every right to be dour: in his own country he is usually worse. In Scotland he may permit the occasional ray of moonlight but the notion of sunshine would escape his psyche.

There are exceptions. One such is Bill Shackleton who has managed to combine a career as a Church of Scotland minister with a rumbustious good humour which has disconcerted both his various congregations and the nation for many years. Thus this latest opus of his, his first foray into the novel, though not fiction. He has been at fiction for decades. In this book you will find indeed a Scottish minister; in fact you will find two and that is for you to find out at that. The reverend Archie McTaggart is a comic creation which I suspect will last for long. The rest of the cast list – his wife Margaret, his mother-in-law, (who I rather liked) and his dreadful sons. One a disastrous GP, the other a cabinet minister – and no matter the calamity a doctor can create it is as nothing to that, according to Archie McTaggart, which a cabinet minister chap can inflict. Then there are the appalling circumstances into which the Rev. Archie finds himself – pop stars, weddings, drink…you will just have to read this for yourself.

What I can tell you is this: mix Tom Sharpe with Para Handy and you get only a little whiff of what is often,

iv

and erroneously said to be a "jaunty Highland romp". There are indeed lots of jaunty Highland romps but they are rarely portrayed in print. A Scot in print is likely to be about as jaunty as a bout of constipation. But Mr Shackleton's tome is indeed jaunty and highland. And it is most decidedly a romp. We must see more of the Rev. Archie McTaggart. He cannot disappear into the Scottish mist and gloom. More, Shaksy, more! And one last cliché. It's Bein' so cheerful as keeps us going.

JACK MCLEAN 2008

Other titles by the same author

Keeping It Cheery
Sunk by my Levity

CHAPTER ONE

A Quiet Life

The Reverend Archie McTaggart stared prayerfully through the window of his study, muttering to himself that he was the luckiest man in the world. He had a happy family, a job which he loved, and here he was with a bird's-eye view from his manse which could not be rivalled for scenic beauty. To crown these pleasurable thoughts, this was Monday morning and a beautiful day for his weekly game of golf with the Laird.

He looked northwards over the wide waters of the Firth to the distant, hazy mountains of Sutherland; turned his gaze up the length of the Firth with its white yachts sailing about like tiny swans, and scanned the vast panorama of Wester Ross, with its far off Highland glens and forests. Bonnie Scotland, indeed - these were scenes which never ceased to please Archie, and the visitors to his many roomed Victorian manse on the hill which overlooked the wee port of St. Regulus, and sheltered it from the cold easterly winds from the North Sea.

The town took its name from the fabled Saint Regulus who brought the bones of St. Andrew to Scotland; after sailing with these relics up and down the east coast, legend records that the saint finally deposited them in the city of St. Andrews, persuaded to do so by the Picts who told him that the golf courses there were better than anywhere else. There are sceptics who doubt this legend, but anyone who asks the few last surviving Picts (now caddies on the Old Course) will be told that the tale is more than true. Be that as it may, Regulus, like the Romans before him, found *Porta Salutis* provided a safe anchorage in the Firth, and left a miniature church there dedicated to his name. From this beginning evolved the present town of St. Regulus.

From his manse lookout point, the Rev. Archie (Erchie to his familiars) could see right below his feet the town's lighthouse on its rocky promontory, the long sandy beach, the broad grassy links skirted by Shore Street, the clustered houses of the parish, the Carnegie Library, the Court House Museum, and the turreted Primary School. A conservation area, in summer tourists came from far and wide by bus and by cruise liners to wander the narrow lanes (vennels) of picturesque St. Regulus, admire its eighteenth century stately merchants' mansions, paint its flowery quaint fisher-town cottages, enjoy its tearooms, and a drink at the Crown Hotel.

They also came to spot the dolphins, unique to British waters, hiring boats to take them out to see these sporting in the Firth, the broad waters of which had seen in years gone by, during wartime, the entire Home Fleet, row after row of mighty battleships, moored safely from German attack. Defended by two fortified, dominating hills, between which runs the deep and narrow channel forming a natural entrance into the Firth, this is the finest anchorage in Europe, capable of taking the largest of vessels. Before the days of modern transport, sailing ships traded (and pirated) from here around the world, their captains bringing their wealth back to the tiny fishing village of St. Regulus to build their fine houses.

Beside the manse, towering over the town is a tall memorial column on which stands a statue of the ancient town's most famous son, the Rev. Dr. Alexander Brown (1750-1822).

A maternal ancestor of the aforementioned Rev. Archie, this "lad o' pairts" was an explorer, cartographer, surveyor, a friend of Benjamin Franklin, and a distinguished lecturer in Natural Philosophy. As a boy in St. Regulus ("Reggie" to the locals), he invented 'the wireless telegraphy', sending messages across the Firth from Castle Sutor, the residence at that period of Lord McSutor, a retired Paymaster of the East India Company who put his fortune into turning the dilapidated castle into Sutor House, his stately home, and building the 18th century stone harbour.

His mind too quick to linger long on any amusing "toy", as he called his invention of the wireless, the young Brown left for a life of adventure in the New World, where he became the first man to cross and map the Rocky Mountains - achieving this feat long before Lewis and Clark travelled coast to coast. He became famously known throughout the colonies as "The Pathfinder", and, after serving as chaplain to George Washington, and adding his signature to the Declaration of Independence, the first of no less than five Universities, twenty colleges, fifteen rivers, and forty-five Brownsvilles began to dot the expanding U.S.A., all named in his honour. The people of "Reggie", justly proud of their town's high reputation in the Land of the Free, took note that their 'meenister' had inherited a generous helping of his illustrious forefather's precious genes, for Erchie was a bright spark.

He was not a tall man (he described himself as being 'well over four feet' in his socks, holes and all) but somehow seemed tall, due to a sturdy frame, a clear voice, forceful presence, and impressive beliefs.

Very much a 'man's man', Archie had been a chaplain to the Royal Marines and so he brought to his ministry a sane realism plus an ability to take people as he found them. Cheerful, witty, popular as a person, respected as a practitioner of what he preached, Archie's favourite Burns quote was: "The man o' independent mind, he looks and laughs at a' that". Scornful of pomposity, he was often deliberately mischievous, leaving people never quite sure whether or not he was being serious. In short (I said he wasn't very tall), Archie was happy to be who and what he was, and, apart from his mother-in-law, nobody could disturb his easy-going nature.

While contemplating the view from the manse, and feeling himself the monarch of all he surveyed, Archie recalled with pleasure how he had recently swum in the Sea of Galilee in the morning and in Firth in the evening of the same day, in so doing fulfilling an ambition and winning a bet with the Marquis. He was snapped out of his reverie, by the horn of the Laird's car blasting out imperiously at his front door, summoning him to fall in for the golf.

The Laird, never called anything other than "The Colonel" by all who knew him, was an eighty year old former commanding officer, who ran his life like a military operation. He saw the world as a war zone and the nearby golf course as a battlefield.

The Colonel, well over six feet tall, straight as a flagpole, craggy, the chinless product of generations of Etonians and Generals, would have been regarded as a somewhat forbidding figure had it not been for the endearing, absent-minded, other-worldliness which tempered his high born bossiness. As the average height of the inhabitants of "Reggie" was five feet six, the Colonel never looked anyone in the eye, and seemed to spend his life squinting over their heads as if on the lookout for approaching enemy aircraft. Every morning he left his ancestral home to appear in the town wearing a kilt and looking as if making his daily inspection of the barracks. Every few steps, he would halt momentarily, stand upright as a piano, and then suddenly take off at the double leaning forwards with his nose stuck out like one of his pointer dogs racing to pick up a downed pheasant. Although considered somewhat remote and disconcertingly unpredictable, the Colonel was popular with one and all. He had no favourites - except one: Archie. He and the minister got on very well together, having taken immediately to each other as soon as they first met in St. Regulus kirk twenty years earlier. The Colonel was Archie's Session Clerk, as well as his golfing partner.

Leaving the manse and climbing into the Colonels' Land Rover, Archie was as happy as any man is entitled to be. He felt 'up for it' – every dog has its day and this, Archie told himself, was his day, the day when he would beat his rival, though it would take some doing for the Colonel was a big hitter and nifty around the greens. The sun shone, God was in His heaven and all was right with the world. Archie hummed the song, "Life's great, life's grand, future's all planned, No more clouds in the sky, how'm I riding? I'm riding high".

The Colonel was much admired by Archie for his loyalty, simplicity, and forthright manner. You knew where you were with him. And he was an excellent golfer and no man like that can be distrusted. Besides, the old boy had an uncanny ability to work miracles with his short game, chipping and putting to a most disconcertingly accurate degree. He possessed what Archie enviously called a "Harry Potter Putter", a club which could hole a put from thirty feet, no bother. Archie, whose golfing skills had been formed on the Local Authority courses of Glasgow, had no greater ambition in life than to return home after playing against the Colonel and answer his wife's inevitable question "Well, who won?" with the wonderful words, "I did, dear".

For his part, the Colonel liked and respected his minister, never addressing him as "Archie", or even Mr. McTaggart, but always "Padre". Both men had been through hard battle experiences of which they never spoke, but which bonded them closely. True, sometimes the Padre's sermons bordered on left-wing views, but the Colonel soon forgot what was said in the pulpit, just as everyone else in the pews did, so no criticisms surfaced. And the padre was always short and interesting, and that was what mattered to the Colonel.

After lunch in the club house, feeling pleased with himself, Archie returned home to an empty house, his wife, Margaret being at work, part-time teaching in the Secondary School some miles away. There was no sign of Sylvia, her mother, which, for Archie was always a good sign. As he picked up his morning mail, he had the satisfaction of knowing that for once he had beaten his 'significant other half' to his letters – wives like to get to a man's letters before he does, a practice which irks husbands no end, but against which they protest in vain.

A wee dram, a long snooze in a hot bath, a stirring hymn sung as he dried himself, life that late afternoon in June could not have been improved upon for the Rev. Archie McTaggart. Then, oblivious to the catastrophe about to befall him, he opened the letters.

CHAPTER TWO

The Letter

He had two letters and the first one added to his happy mood as it contained an invitation to toast the Immortal Memory at the Burns Club of Singapore – for the third time. Nice to be appreciated and Archie was a well-known, far travelled after-dinner speaker in great demand, especially at Burns Suppers, St. Andrew's Nights, and Royal Marine Reunions.

Archie was a "clubbable man" of the kind which the Great Panjandrum himself would have approved, and it is not difficult to picture him spending convivial evenings at The Literary Club passing the port with Joshua Reynolds, Oliver Goldsmith, Edmund Burke, and David Garrick. Robert Burns was Archie's hero. Books were his treasure; and the great humorist writers from Charles Lamb to P. G. Wodehouse were his daily spiritual companions. Without so much as looking at the date, he wrote a letter straightaway saying he would be delighted to speak in Singapore.

Picking up his second letter, he saw it bore the crest of the House of Commons; it was from his elder son, Gordon. Archie did not have a lot of time for politicians, but he was proud of Gordon, a member of the Cabinet, a young man who had made the name McTaggart known in high places and was tipped as favourite runner in the P.M. Stakes. Opening it, he read as follows....

"Dear Dad,

You won't believe this (I know you never believe politicians) but I am about to move into No.10, you-know-where–street. It hasn't been issued to the Press yet, so keep mum – especially

13

keep Mum from telling her friends and Granny Sylvia, or it will be all over the county and newspapers. I am waiting to leak it at the best time to get my own back on the B.B.C. for putting it round I am a homosexual just because I'm thirty-four and a bachelor. They think I am one of them, the leeches.

There is another reason for keeping it secret – hang on to your hat! I am getting married! You always said I should find a nice girl to caddy for me in the round of life (remember that sermon you preached on "Marriage and the Fairways of Life"), well I've found one. She is so like Mum it isn't true – same loving, talented, ideal wife for a man. You'll like her.

She is in Las Vegas just now, but as soon as she gets back we want to come up to St. Regulus and have you marry us. Her name is Annie O'Hara and we first met at an Embassy Reception in Washington. You will know her better by her stage name Magdalene. She is a great entertainer as you know. Will being an American make much difference to having a wedding in Scotland? She is SO keen to being married there because you can conduct the wedding, and she had a Scottish great-grandmother. We decided against her home town of Brownsville, West Virginia, because a British P.M. being married in the U.S.A. would not go down well politically here, and I have to consider very carefully the high security risks involved.

Magdalene has been widowed, remarried and had that marriage annulled by the Vatican – will that make any difference to you, Dad? I hope not. All we want a quiet wedding in the old St.Regulus' kirk I know so well. We realize that given her celebrity and my high profile just now, it is hardly going to be possible to keep out the publicity, so we must maintain the utmost discretion. I will be in touch as soon as I can. Till then, do keep it dark.

In haste, your loving son,
Gordon."

14

To say this letter had a profound effect upon Archie would be the biggest understatement since Moses wrote describing his own death. He stood awhile shaken by its contents. Indeed, his thoughts were so agitated that he went outside into the manse garden to calm his nerves by practicing his short game, but his concentration was so badly affected that he sliced several of his wedge shots, and left his chips consistently short. This depressingly bad play further irritated his already highly disturbed emotions, and so it was that upon his wife's return it was with a troubled mind that he silently handed the letter over to Margaret before she had time to take off her coat, put down her briefcase, and ask what was for tea.

It would be no exaggeration to say that after reading Gordon's news, she was so stunned that she stood wordless for the first time in her life. Then, as Archie anticipated, a verbal explosion followed - "Has he gone mad?" Mum shrieked!

Her husband's erudition was widely recognised and admired, but his knowledge had never extended into the world of Pop music. He had seen this Magdalene dame on the T.V. news, but knew next to nothing about his future daughter-in-law beyond the fact that she was a famous singer and a questionably suitable wife for a Prime Minister of Great Britain and Northern Ireland. But if Archie knew little about his son's fiancée, his spouse did – she knew plenty and that right well from her studies of the pages of the glossy woman's magazines.

If her son had affianced himself to Bin Laden's daughter, Margaret could not have been more displeased. With many words she assailed the ears of her husband, every syllable uncomplimentary as to the character, morals, and provocatively immodest dress-sense of Magdalene - a female who would soon, God forbid, be entering into her family circle. Women being by nature temperamental (50% temper and 50% mental) Archie thought it wise under the circumstances not to point out that forthcoming events were out of their control—they couldn't prevent Gordon marrying whomsoever he chose. So, being a resourceful man, trained to act quickly and decisively in combat, he kept his mouth shut. It would take some sharp thinking to deal with this turn up for the book.

If there was one thing Archie was very good at it was sharp thinking under stress. His famous son had grown up in a manse wherein stress management came with being a member of a busy family directed by a busy father and a busy mother. Gordon grew up being told to get on with things; his competence to do so was never doubted by his parents. English commentators use just two pejorative words to describe a 'son of the manse': he is 'dour', and 'Calvinist' - Gordon got both labels from the London press. But the reality is that 'sons of the manse' are notorious for being young tearaways until, like Gordon, good breeding and a Presbyterian upbringing eventually turn them into cheerful and extremely useful members of society. Margaret and Archie's two sons were clever and anything but 'dour'.

From his mother Gordon got his pleasant looks, direct manner, rounded education, and insights into human nature. From his father he learnt how to lead from the front and get the best out of people; also from Archie he acquired the skills of evasion and obfuscation - always in a good cause, of course - which had helped him climb to the top of the greasy pole of politics. Although affecting to despise politicians, Archie was pretty astute at the management of affairs - "as wise as a serpent, and harmless as a dove" being his Scriptural advice to Gordon for achieving quiet, successful effectiveness.

One of Gordon's most instructive memories was of the time his mother ordered a film for the ladies of Woman's Guild (this powerful organization was steered by the most formidable female in the parish, Margaret McTaggart). Her rival was the Laird's wife, Lady Cynthia, a haughty person who, accustomed to obedience, never ceased to press claims to dominance over the minister's wife, the town, and Guild affairs. C of E from the squirearchy of Berkshire, Cynthia (known for short locally as 'Sin') did not accompany her kilted husband to the kirk on Sundays but made her way instead to a place of worship known locally as 'The English Church' which had, as Robert Burns said of Lamington kirk, 'in't but few', incomers who had sold up in the South to buy cheaply in the North. Seeking a wider audience for her views and presence than these exiles offered, Cynthia deigned to attend Guild meetings in the kirk in order to serve God in what she considered to be an advisory capacity.

Margaret McTaggart had neither forgiven nor forgotten the day of her arrival in the manse some twenty years previously when her ladyship had presented a bundle of her old clothes as a welcoming gift for the new minister's wife. As the donor's height and girth exceeded those of Mrs McTaggart by some twelve inches, the ill-fitting gift was declined with icy politeness as her rival intended it would be.

Forewarned, thereafter the minister's wife made sure that she 'out-ladied' her Ladyship at every joust, to the admiration of the ladies of the town, and the blanket-chewing jealousy of 'Sin'. Being bested privately and publicly by one she does not consider to be her equal is not something a Laird's wife, with a hundred acres of property, can live with, and the business of the film show afforded the Chatelaine of Sutor House an opportunity to put the social order right again in the community.

The film was to have been an educational movie about a school for girls in the Congo, a laudable subject for instruction and missionary inspiration. To a dimmed hall full of hatted ladies, the screen soon revealed that the wrong film had been delivered. What is called a 'hard-core' Swedish pornographic production opened up before the widening eyes of the audience—naked young men and women doing what nature intended in a sunny meadow. With an aggregate number of children and grandchildren reaching up to three figures, sex was not something with which the Guild members were unfamiliar, but they had always thought of it as an indoor rather than an outdoor pursuit. After the film was allowed to continue for longer than protest ought to have allowed, giggles ignited much unrestrained laughter amongst the ladies and excited cries of "Leave it" rang out as the flustered male projectionist moved to shut the show down. It was, the Guild members later said amongst themselves, 'a rare wee night' – although qualifying such approval with a fitting number of "tut-tuts". The main beneficiaries of this 'rare wee night' were the husbands of the town who were pleasantly surprised at how greatly rejuvenated their lady loves were by experiencing the first Hen Night ever held by the Woman's Guild of St. Regulus' kirk.

Explanations as to the mix up over the film were due from the minister's wife, but investigations proving unsatisfactory, Mrs. McTaggart decided the best policy would be to let the whole matter fade away from memory without comment. However, such a juicy tale of debauchery at the Guild afforded her enemy, the Colonel's wife, a great chance to make an anonymous telephone call to the national press embroidering it into a male stripper's performance, along the lines of 'The Full Monty". What swiftly followed taxed the minister's powers of sharp, political prevarication to the full…

Phone call to the manse:-

"Hello, is that Rev. McTaggart?"

"The Rev. Archie McTaggart, if you please—Rev. McTaggart is a vulgar Americanism, but carry on."

"Sorry, Reverend, this is The Express."

"The Express—that will be the Express Laundry and Dry Cleaners."

"No, we're not a laundry….the Express—the newspaper."

"Not the laundry – a newspaper? The Express?—is that like The Scotsman? or The Herald? or The Press & Journal?"

"We are a national not a local newspaper, Vicar. I'm calling from London – I believe you had a pornographic film at a church ladies' meeting up there in Scotland. Are our readers to take it that you approve of pornography?"

"Did you say the ladies at the Guild have had a pornographic film show? I haven't heard about that. Are you sure? I believe they showed a very nice picture recently called 'Seven Persons for Seven Persons'.

"I think you mean 'Seven Brides for Seven Husbands', Sir."

"Yes, that's it—we are very particular here about gender equality and political correctness, we try to keep up with the times. I haven't seen the film myself but I am told it was shot in Sweden with Gaelic sub-titles for folk like us in the Highlands. I believe it is very good. Nice of you people down there to take an interest in us up here—we live such a remote and unexciting life compared to you in the big city down there."

"We had a telephone call saying the film was disgusting and filthy and a disgrace. What do you say to that, Father McTaggart?"

"Ah, that would be the anonymous telephone call from Her Ladyship."

"You know about it, Vicar?"

"Oh yes, she does that sort of thing, poor old soul. Confused you see, senile dementia, terrible thing, she likes to write anonymous letters to people. We all understand."

It was in conversations such as these that the minister of St. Regulus displayed that capacity for good natured prevarication, which his eldest son Gordon had, from his infancy, learnt the arts of good government.

After receipt of the letter with its bombshell news, Mr. McTaggart left his fretting wife at the tea table and headed down into the town's newspaper shop for his copies of Golf Monthly and The Expository Times. Passers-by detected in his somewhat muted response to their greetings that their minister had something weighing on his mind, and they were right: Erchie was worried and furtive.

CHAPTER THREE

Doctors & Dilemmas

If the word leaked out that the next P.M. was marrying a woman who was, Archie's distraught wife assured him, a pop idol of immense wealth and dubious reputation, where would that lead? He shuddered to think of hordes of paparazzi invading St. Regulus (Archie never called it "Reggie"), brazenly taking photographs through the manse windows day and night. The prospect terrified him. And there was his own reputation to consider – how could he marry a female, celebrity or no celebrity, whose marriage had been annulled by the Vatican – divorce by wealth and stealth Archie called it scornfully. Who had annulled who, and why? He was a liberal-minded man – he had married divorcées before, but duty required him to be cautious.

The time when he married a couple who forgot to tell him how OFTEN they had each been divorced had made him wary – these were a couple seemingly worth a second chance, and before the wedding they told him they were divorced right enough, but what they omitted to do was tell the minister until after the wedding that each of them had been divorced five times! Archie could have written a book about the number of times he had been given false names, met underage girls giving a false date of birth, brides making off with the best man after a reception in a posh hotel. You couldn't be too careful. As with weddings, so also with burials; people laughed when Archie told them that he always looked at the name on the brass plate on the coffin lid so he could be sure the person inside was who he thought it to be. Such was life these days – take nothing at face value.

Another thought struck Archie: what religion was this American female pop celebrity bidding to become his daughter-in-law? He shuddered to recall the memory of the hippy commune which had flourished within the boundaries of his parish, a settlement of bearded, sandaled, grinning young males, surrounded by earnest young women dressed like Pocahontas and dancing around singing about appeasement and justice. Happily, their stay only lasted until their zeal for Hari Krishna dwindled away, and they moved on to warmer climes more convenient to the social security offices than St. Regulus. Pop stars lead modern youth into the drug culture and sexual promiscuity, so was Magdalene another weirdo: a Moonie, a Scientologist, one of these Rastafarians, a Five-and-a-Half-day-week-Adventist, or something like that? Naw! No way, he dismissed such thoughts because Gordon, who never went out without a suit and a tie, would never marry somebody like that; image, respectability these were his big thing. Archie felt reassured, but then, on second thoughts, you never know, for he knew that he had been richt weel suckered before. He would have to watch it.

Doubts rarely fermented in Archie's spirit but they were doing so more and more now. He already had one son whose sanity was questionable; could his elder son, the rock on which the Labour Party's hopes were founded, be going the same way as his younger brother? Why on earth would Gordon want to marry such a *femme fatal* as Magdalene? Archie had long presumed that G. B. Shaw was right to describe life as "one damned thing after another", and here he was receiving ample evidence to prove it. The questions mounted up and the answers did not amount to much.

It began to rain as he walked uphill home, regretting he had come out without his umbrella. Things could not get worse, he mused, but he was wrong about that. As he fiddled for his keys, a seagull dive bombed his new cap, screeched with laughter, and flew off at speed to share the joke with the local bird life.

Mum greeted her husband's return with the news that Dr. Fry had called to say that she was leaving for a summer holiday month on her native Jura, the island on which she annually housed herself amidst twenty thousand deer, billions of ferocious midges, and a few hardy perennial whisky distillers. This was not good news for Archie. It was, in fact, bad news for it implied that once again, Dr Fry had invited their younger son, Arthur, to replace her as locum.

Pleasing though it would be to see their flesh and blood for a couple of months, memories of his last spell as locum at the surgery did not augur well for the future. The previous year, the youthful, hyper-active Doc. Arthur had blown into town like a whirlwind and well and truly put the wind up the townsfolk who had no idea they were ill until after he had examined them. He revelled in detecting rare diseases and discovering new ones, often speaking feelingly of his disappointment that his home town had not provided him with a single death from bubonic plague. Parental guidance during his formative years had not diverted Arthur's misdirected enthusiasms into the paths of peace, and the news of his imminent arrival burdened the sorely tried souls of his mum and dad with much apprehension.

Not that the people of the town and surrounding farms were unused to receiving the services of an eccentric physician for Dr. Fry herself was an odd ball. If women can be catalogued under three heading: birds, puddings, and horses, Madge Fry would be filed under the last of these three. She had very long legs, and, when stooping, a back which would have fitted a saddle perfectly. It would be unkind to say that her face usually bore the expression of a disdainful camel, but the comparison has been drawn by the unkind. However, her unprepossessing appearance concealed a benevolent nature and, as her personal eccentricities leaned on virtue's side, Dr. Fry was accepted by everyone. Fate having consigned them into Madge's care, the sick were resigned to trusting their one and only available G.P., though keenly aware of the risks involved in taking her unconventional remedies. Like everything else in slow moving "Reggie", the good doctor fitted in because, as everyone said philosophically, time is the great healer.

A spinster of indeterminate years, Dr. Fry had practised in St. Regulus ever since qualifying at Glasgow University. The story was that, having failed repeatedly, she had passed the exams only because the examiner had happened to be away at the time when he usually marked her papers. On his return, while walking past her newly opened surgery and seeing her name on the brass plate, the man had panicked to think she had been let loose upon the sick and dying due to his absence at the marking. It was with relief he heard that she had set up shop in far distant St. Regulus, and, after a few warnings to fellow reputable sawbones of his acquaintance in the North, he had let it go at that. It was his consolation to know that the main centres of population were safe.

It has to be said that Dr. Fry was most attentive to her patients. When she was pulled up by her superiors for over prescribing, everyone knew that she was only doing so to provide her six horses, three dogs, and innumerable cats with necessary anti-biotics, and they vigorously defended her against reproach. Her diagnoses and treatments certainly surprised those who consulted her,

24

but they made for good gossip. When Big Jock the Plumber called at the surgery with a bad back, he was asked if he took a drink; apologetically he mumbled that he occasionally took "a wee refreshment". Expecting to be caned for touching strong drink, it came as a great surprise to hear Dr Fry say, "You should take a good drink; taking a bucket will be good for you." Disappointment followed, however, when she did not write out a prescription for a bottle of whisky, which was a pity because he would have found it useful as evidence of her medical treatment for a bad back.

"What do you think of that?" said a disconcerted Big Jock as he recounted the tale to all on his job rounds; "Imagine a doctor telling you take a good drink!" Ladies whose kitchen sinks he un-choked, together with his cronies in the 'Crown' tap bar, needed little persuasion to believe it for many other stories of their doctor's prescriptive abnormalities were in circulation. However, the case of their friendly neighbourhood plumber particularly interested the local householders because Big Jock was the only man who knew where all the pipes went underground in the ancient borough and therefore how to fix them. An alcoholic plumber they did not want around, especially in winter when they had bursts requiring emergency repair.

It was a well-known fact that the doctor was not one of those people who ask others to do what she was not prepared to do herself. In other words, Dr. Fry sometimes took "a good bucket". This was unusual in a lady who occupied the exalted post of Secretary to the Women's Guild for many years, but St. Regulus was an unusual place, as incomers soon discovered.

On her arrival as the new parish minister's wife, Margaret became Guild President and was told on the quiet of her Secretary's fondness for a tipple. During the tea following a Guild meeting, the church officer, Jim Strong by name, arrived smelling strongly (not for the first time) of strong drink. Clasping Dr. Fry to his bosom, he emotional addressed her with the words: "Madge Fry, you are a wonderful woman". His advances were not as speedily rejected by their Secretary as the ladies present expected. Her breath smelling of peppermint, the doctor did not look entirely averse to the close encounter, and for a few moments it was unclear who was clasping who. On much closer inspection, Jim realized that Madge Fry was not the Venus he had observed at a distance and managed to struggle free of the embrace. The upshot of all this was that the Kirk Session removed him from office following complaints from the more prudish amongst the Guild members.

Still in the prime of life, Jim was quite a good looking, exceptionally fit chap and everyone in the town noticed, with knowing winks, that in the years following the above reported incident, Dr. Fry was often seen paying house calls to his bachelor home late at night for reasons which could not be considered to have anything to do with his health. The McTaggarts were quite fond of their doctor, in a reserved sort of way, Margaret showing her how to cook simple meals, and Archie turning a blind eye to her illicit assignations on the reasonable grounds that he could do nothing about them. The minister of St. Regulus took a tolerant, Presbyterian view of sexual relationships amongst his parishioners, for it was his experience and belief that nature sorts things out in the long run and they usually did.

Arthur's parents had no reservations at all about the undesirability of their son coming to take up Madge's stethoscope. A handsome thirty year old spring chicken of a bachelor, brimming with boundless vitality, exhaustingly cheerful, and fit as an orchestra of fiddles, the appointment meant in Arthur's eyes an opportunity for him to bounce around the practice unintentionally embarrassing his parents once again. Dr. Arthur meant well, that none could deny, but memories of his locumship the previous year burnt brightly in the memories of Archie, Margaret, and their fellow citizens.

One story, most widely known and relished because it was a town secret, was when the baker's wife sought a cure for a troublesome feminine complaint requiring the use of a vaginal cream. Unfortunately, Dr. Arthur had forgotten that in "Reggie" everyone has what is quaintly called 'a bye-name', that is a nickname used by everyone except by its owner, and never to be spoken in his or her presence. To further confuse anyone unacquainted with this inexplicable, time-honoured practice; the baker's wife had two bye-names (why nobody could even guess): "Sibby" and "Gigger". The end result was Dr. Arthur dashing off careless prescriptions for vaginal cream for two non-existent women and issuing the baker's wife with a prescription for a muscle pain ointment which heated affected areas. When his patient applied this fiery substance to her tender private parts, her shrieks were loud and long. Following a slow, painful, and partial recovery, the baker's wife was left inflamed with anger and a burning desire to shove Dr. Arthur into her husband's oven, and she would have done so had not movement on her part involved the reigniting of her nether regions.

On the last day of his locumship in the previous year, Dr. Arthur called at Sutor House after hearing that Lady Cynthia was 'unwell'. Eager to begin diagnosis and treatment of whatever ailed the patient, he arrived at 7a.m., and, finding her in bed beside her startled husband, cheerfully flung back the covers, lifted Cynthia's nightie over her head, took her blood pressure, then her temperature (anally), poked around at her naked abdomen and concluded his examination by shaking his head from side to side and pronouncing solemnly that this was a case of infectious Hepatitis B. Her Ladyship, lying in a state of nudeness never before seen by His Lordship at close quarters, trembled with shock, rendered speechless for once in her life by surprise and acute embarrassment. As quickly as he had arrived, the doctor quarantined his gasping, recumbent patient, scribbled out a prescription, promised a speedy return, and left His Lordship to avert his eyes from what was not a pretty sight while gurgling, "Bless my soul!"

During the course of that, his last morning, Dr. Arthur diagnosed a further six cases of Hepatitis B, quarantining each house involved. By the time he was driving away back to Glasgow, the shops of the town were deserted as word flew round that there was a pandemic of deadly Hepatitis spreading rapidly. Doors were bolted, blinds drawn, cats and dogs left to roam the empty, forlorn streets. News of the dire situation reaching the Medical Officer of Health, a team of gloved and masked medical personnel arrived, and found that not only was Lady Cynthia in good health, but so were all the other cases of suspected Hepatitis. Such was the relief in the town at this happy conclusion (ascribed by the more religiously inclined to a miracle), that no resentment was held against the popular young doctor who began it all, largely because the story of how Her Ladyship was laid out starkers soon circulated, greatly amusing the townsfolk, and bringing admiration and credit to her departed physician. As the M.O.H. was a pal of Arthur's from University days, no more was officially reported of St. Regulus' pestilence and

28

the episode was closed. This spared the blushes of the townsfolk at the time, but left them fearful that one day Dr. Arthur would return with healing diseases known and unknown on his mind. When the news was out from Dr. Fry that he was in fact coming back as her locum once again Lady Cynthia fainted with anxiety.

The next morning, Arthur arrived in his two-seater, M.G. Spitfire, its owner's pride and joy. He tooted his horn vigorously to alert and summon mater and pater then leapt out to hug them closely with many gleeful words of greeting. Like a shot he went indoors leaving them on the front step to follow him into the manse...

"Great news, eh, Dad?" beamed Arthur, as he made himself a pot of tea in the kitchen. "Gordie, getting hitched, and guess who is the Best Man? Me! Waken the old place up a bit when Magdalene swoops in and, boy it sure needs wakening up!"

Dad groaned and swore - "Damn it! Damn it and blast it!" Archie often swore, mildly let it be said. As an infant the family had lived next door to an old Irishman who gave him a penny for every new swear word he learnt. By the time his horrified mother intervened, he has accumulated a basic vocabulary and an independent income. "Damn it!" he repeated with increased emphasis - If Arthur knew about this wedding, who else did?

Mother was not a woman given to hysterics, or displays of distress, but during the course of the above brief conversation she suddenly fled upstairs into the bedroom sobbing.

"What's up?" asked Arthur, "she seems almost upset."

"Upset! Upset! Of course she is upset. Your brother loses his mind and goes off with a blasted American bimbo from the Pop Shows…"

"Concerts, father, they call them, Pop Concerts or Gigs," said Arthur interposing and correcting in his ever helpful way.

His father closed his eyes, and moaned in the sort of a despairing voice which a man uses when he has just dropped six strokes getting out of a bunker. Son number two, hearing but not listening, had fixed his attention on the fridge door.

"It isn't shutting properly, Dad, I'll nip out to the car and get my toolbox." Archie, remembering how on his last visit Arthur had dismantled the washing machine and left the bits lying about for three weeks, hastened to curb his son's D.I.Y. enthusiasm. "Leave the bloody thing alone," he commanded, "don't you dare touch it.", and so saying he turned on his heel and marched into the study deserting the bewildered Arthur who was left scratching his head and asking himself - "What's got into the old man?"

It did not take long for Mother to move from the frantic to the grim silence and therein to recover her self-control and composure. While Archie paced up and down in his study, she was on the telephone to New York where, the British Embassy informed her, Gordon was lecturing the U.N. on foreign policy. He was unavailable to take the call; Margaret was much displeased she had much to say to son Gordon, and she had been planning on giving him an overdue earful of it. As boys, her sons had learnt that their loving Mum, when provoked, possessed a left hook to the jaw worthy of Mohammed Ali and when her wrath was aroused they treated her wishes with circumspection.

Age had not wearied Margaret Sinclair nor the years condemned: her petite figure had not inclined either to skinniness, or to fatness. Still a good looking woman, always smartly dressed, Margaret was ever attentive to her appearance, enhancing her presence with a sunshine personality, intelligent brown eyes, and educated conversation. She was what her husband called in awe and admiration - "all woman", and he adored her in that shy, reticent manner which characterizes the Scottish male and which the English mistake for dourness.

Her sons had inherited their mother's looks and, in her elder son's case, her common sense, shrewdness, and poise. Younger son Arthur certainly had her brains, but not her cool glandular system. Arthur's blood had been overheated from his infancy, a misfortune for which his mother blamed her husband's brother, Donald, a certifiably insane Edinburgh architect whose *neo alcoholic* designs for the new Scottish Parliament had come very close to rapturous approval. Anxious to stop his uncle's plans for the sort of massive building which would not only have cost the earth but covered a good deal of it, Gordon quickly used his heavy Labour Party clout to stop the disastrous project before it could begin, thus saving the nation from a hideous *'Germania'*, or Batman's *'Gotham City'* look-alike which may have accorded well with his uncle's nightmare's and Hitler's architectural fantasies, but not with the Royal Mile, or, for that matter, with Gordon's political ambitions. If a new parliament building was required, then let others put up a folly and damage their political prospects - Gordon did not want his reputation sullied by accusations of nepotism, and the ruination of Scotland's architectural heritage.

Margaret's suspicions that there was a streak of insanity in the McTaggart blood extended beyond brother-in-law Donald, and son Arthur, to her very own spouse Archie who, on one occasion, astonished her and the congregation by booting a rugby ball into the gallery of the kirk shouting, "That's the first conversion of the New Year." Such scenes convinced Margaret that she had married into a family of loonies. Admittedly, it was biologically difficult to prove but she was compensated by the belief that her first born, her sensible Gordon, although fathered by Archie, had not a drop of fevered McTaggart blood in his veins coming, as he did, exclusively from her side of the family: the sane Sinclairs.

For his part, Archie had his own theories as to the origins of his younger son's eccentricity – he blamed the endocrine glands of his father-in-law, a man who was, in Archie's considered opinion, anything but mentally stable. His wife's view that her Sinclair relatives were exemplars of sweet reasonableness was not one he shared with her. For instance, her father seemed to be under the impression, drawn from a book called "The Da Vinci Code", that the Sinclairs were descended from the Earls of Orkney, the Knights Templar, and the marriage of Mary Magdalene to Jesus Christ. When he pointed out to Margaret that her father was completely cuckoo, she forcefully defended this absurd genealogical theory. Wives feel obliged to contradict their husbands (it is with them a matter of principle) so Archie, expecting her to take her Daddy's part in any dispute, didn't take her seriously, but once he began to think about her strangely over-the-top reaction to Gordon's fiancée's name being Magdalene the more he suspected that 'his 'significant other' saw connections to her family tree which only a dotty Sinclair could see.

Having fallen for his future wife at University in Glasgow, Archie visited the home of her parents in Orkney for the purpose of asking her father for his daughter's hand in marriage – a courtesy nowadays believed to be as outdated as marriage itself, but at that period required and approved. A ten hour drive brought him to John o' Groats where he boarded a small vessel, and, after surviving a terrifying crossing of the whirlpools and mountainous seas of the perilous Pentland Firth (on a lovely summer's evening at that), Archie finally arrived at the door of a lonely, black, spooky stone house which would have made the ideal set for the filming of "Wuthering Heights".

Standing in the gloaming with the shadows lengthening, feeling the chill of falling night, he hammered on the door until it slowly creaked open to reveal the mother of his beloved Margaret. It was a, slender, smaller woman than he had imagined who materialised out of the dark interior dressed in a white nightgown, carrying an oil lamp and looking frighteningly like the ghost of a demented Florence Nightingale. Without welcome or introduction, this apparition led him by the light of the lamp into a sitting-room, there, presumably, to await the arrival of her husband, Dr. Sinclair.

They sat in silence, Archie's occasional polite sallies into conversation proving to be like playing tennis with nobody returning your serves. The large blank spaces in the non-existent small talk gave him ample time to look at his surroundings and in the dim light on offer he noted that the floor was only half covered with linoleum tiles, and that the only furniture in the room consisted of three dining room chairs, and a coffee table. Archie tried to stir things up a bit by asking if she and her husband were in the process of flitting and either moving out or moving into the house, but the brief answer he received indicated that they had been in occupation for many years and had no wish to leave their happy home. Stacked up cases of provisions lined the walls and corridors, as if the Sinclairs were about to embark on an Artic expedition. Archie's chair was not conducive to comfort and lengthy occupancy. He kept shifting about and, when not counting his teeth with his tongue for the hundredth time, kept shaking his watch to see if it had stopped.

Midnight coming with no sign of his future father-in-law, or explanations to his whereabouts, the lady with the lamp suddenly arose and led him up a stone staircase to his bedroom, the furnishing of which was as sparse as that in the sitting-room below. There was a comfy single bed, but neither chair nor hook to hang his clothes, nor curtains for the windows. It was with fearful doubts that he might not survive the night that he turned in, dreading the thought that he might have to leave the room during the wee small hours for a wee-wee in some haunted bathroom far away.

Always an early riser from his military habit, Archie sat down to await a breakfast of porridge, the production of which by his hostess took several hours, and was so well cooked that it had flattened and hardened into what appeared to be a kippered herring resistant to penetration by spoon, fork and knife. Gazing at it Archie wondered if his future wife had learnt how to cook from her mother - and felt tremors of alarm. These were dispersed, and he was delivered from the polite necessity of attempting to eat this stuff, by the late morning arrival of Margaret and, some time later, of her elusive old man who showed up from somewhere.

The doctor was as tall as his wife was small, looked like a slightly tipsy Abraham Lincoln, and proved pleasantly voluble. His manifestation had a transforming effect on the little woman (still in her white nightdress) and she started to talk a very great deal at high speed, from which Archie gathered her name was Sylvia. With Margaret beaming her usual enchanting smiles, and the sun shining on the finest day ever known in Orkney, Archie started to feel that his prospects for a successful visit were improving, that is they were until his Dad to be, offered to take him for a drive round the islands and the linking 'barrages' installed by Mr. Churchill.

Archie followed the cadaverous figure of Doc. Sinclair out to a barn, the two big wooden doors of which he helped open to reveal an L-plated old Ford occupied by chickens. These having been chased out, and the missing back seat reinstalled, Archie asked if Mrs. Sinclair was about to take her driving test, only to be answered that it was, in fact, the Doc. himself who was about to do so - for the ninth time! "Hop in," ordered the cheerful driver, and off Archie set on one of the most hair-raising experiences of his life - although battle-hardened by shot and shell, he had never been subjected to such a terrifying ordeal before.

The doctor could not change gear, and much of their journey was passed in reverse. It was no consolation to Archie to be told that his driver had been injured on two occasions in crashes with some of the heavy lorries which they were only passing unscathed on the narrow roads by the grace of God. Doctor Fry kept her death count confined within the surgery, but here, in the great outdoors, Archie feared he was now being driven directly into the hereafter by a General Practitioner he hardly knew. The bumpy journey seemed endless: the sun 'did not hasten to go down for a whole day' (see Joshua 10:13) and his chauffeur's exultant enjoyment of every moment did nothing to get it moving. In his student days Archie had shared a long table at college with a dozen medical students, and concluded they were all mentally ill, and here he was now, about to marry a woman fathered by a crazy sawbones.

Margaret's mother was obviously not plumb either, and she seemed to have taken an irrational, instant and deep dislike of Archie (her credal belief was that her daughter should marry into money). So, all in all, the result of his visit was that Archie resolved to marry Margaret as speedily as possible so that he need never return to her parents' lair again. That his son Arthur became a doctor, and was dubiously sane, Archie had no difficulty in understanding after having met Margaret's medicine-man father. Needless to say, he made no mention of this to his dear wife for reasons of personal protection.

If Arthur was a disappointment to his father (Archie thought his boy too clever to be a doctor, and not mad enough to be a Marine) then to even things up Margaret took pride in the fact that their son Gordon, being a Libran like herself, was a well balanced, dependable, and mature individual. Gordon was noted in his high profile public life for his prudence and competence, so his mother had no doubts that he would straighten out this wedding business for her once he turned up. That could not happen soon enough, for the whole thing was making her lose her cool and at odds with Archie. The idea of her Gordon marrying this Magdalene, a creature from another planet, was so outlandish and totally improbable that it must be a joke – a very bad joke, but a joke at that. Yet she knew it was no joke – Gordon was the last person to joke. And it was so unlike Gordon not to have 'phoned her, so very unlike him.

She left a tart, mother's message at the U.N. for him to 'phone her back as soon as possible, and withdrew to give further thought to her next step.

Some things were clear: firstly, Archie couldn't possibly conduct the wedding of an annulled woman – Margaret was determined about that and Margaret could be very determined when she determined to be. He wasn't doing it; that was that.

A life-long Orcadian Liberal, she disapproved of her elder son's Socialist leanings and often told him so when he took them to lunch in Whitehall. In Margaret's veins ran Free Kirk blood, circulating with the red, white, and blue cells of generations of hardy seagoing folk who had fished the waters off Greenland, crewed lifeboats, and sailed the seven seas before the mast. Her beloved Granny had rounded Cape Horn no less than seven times in a windjammer (Archie joked her captain husband couldn't find his way home). With such an ancestry, Margaret Gunn Sinclair McTaggart had the sea in her blood, and with or without a Bible in her hand she could be a very determined person indeed.

Definitely no wedding, definitely…however, on second thoughts, further reflection, and deeper consideration – it began to occur to Margaret that a wedding might not be too bad after all. There was an upside as well as a down…after all, her son was proposing to marry a great celebrity. The whole world would be looking on. St. Regulus kirk would become a Westminster Abbey; Church Street magically turn into The Mall. This was Cinderella territory and Margaret was right in it, her childhood dreams come true!

The female mind is not slow to recognise opportunities when they providentially appear - a new outfit – the right hat – Margaret pictured herself in that exorbitantly expensive dress she had seen in Inverness. She began to brighten up: there would be a sunny day, admiring crowds, envious eyes, the reception with famous guests, and there was that sad young widow with two wee ones in the Sunday School who would be really delighted if they were the lovely flower girls and that would give the whole town a lift – the outlook for this wedding grew brighter and brighter. She regretted her hasty remarks decrying Magdalene's character; she felt sure now that Magdalene was very nice person and they would get along very well once they actually met…when you actually come face to face with someone, person to person, well, as she had often said, it is quite different woman to woman.

It must have been very hard for Magdalene to be widowed so young and after a brief married life. And no doubt her second marriage had broken down because her husband had been bad to her – seeing what men are, some of them anyway – and then girls get carried away with romance when they are young and rush into thing…Magdalene deserved all the sympathy a wronged woman is due…besides, there wasn't a rule which actually forbade Archie giving them a church marriage…and even if there was such a rule, then there shouldn't be. Such were Margaret's thought processes on the subject of Gordon's intended and her need for a good husband. Although she had entertained other matrimonial plans for Gordon, the choice was his.

In his study, alone and reviewing the situation in a more composed frame of mind, her husband had definitely decided he could not, indeed positively would not, take this wedding. Not even for Gordon. That was final.

Weddings were the bane of Archie's life, they were worse than funerals because they went on so long. And they were always on a Saturday when he could be playing golf, or wanting to go to the football, or watching the rugby on the television; as he often had occasion to ruefully observe to his cronies, people are so inconsiderate of others these days. No golf meant leaving his pals the Colonel, Big Willie, and Tam Smith without a partner in the four-ball medal so he wasn't being selfish about these blasted weddings - other innocent's also suffered. The more Archie dwelt on this melancholy subject, the more he felt overcome with sadness, but then there are times in life when you just have to make the best of things. Births, marriages and death are unavoidable and a parish minister cannot avoid the hatches, matches, and dispatches try as he may.

Just the other Saturday morning, when he buried Maisie the Milk, it rained heavily during the committal at the graveside and after the Service as they waded back to the cars through the mud he had said to Big Willie (who pushed the old dame's milk cart round the streets for her), "Och, well, Willie, we couldnae have played the day in this weather anyway." These *bon mots* left Willie (a 12 handicapper) feeling no drier but a wee bit less resentful at Maisie's choice of a Saturday for her burial. As Archie sat back in his study armchair, tracing these wandering thoughts from funerals to Gordon's connubial intentions, he said to himself philosophically: "Every shroud has a silver lining".

It was at this point that Margaret joined him, wearing a disarming smile and bringing him a sweet sherry...... '*timeo Danaos et dona ferentes*'. She's after something, he immediately thought, and he was right.

At college, it had been the sage advice of his Professor of Old Testament, Jimmy Stewart, to put a bolt on the study door; Jimmy would have a quiet, confidential word on the subject with his students saying, "Wives, like to come in to see what you are doing, or to bring you in something. It breaks your concentration. They burst in on you and want to talk – they can't help it." This Archie had found to be very true, but he had never put a bolt on his study door. A wife feels strongly that in her house "no go areas" are impermissible and Archie yielded the point, knowing that even the elderly professor had lacked the courage to barricade himself in against his wife's intrusions, so what chance had a young husband? A bolt on the study door was one of those great ideas whose time has not yet come.

When Margaret wanted something from Archie she got it. He knew full well that though a husband is head of the house, the wife is the neck which turns it in whatever direction she wishes. Addressing her defensive and grumpy husband, Margaret said, "Archie, this wedding - I think we will have to go through with it." He promptly and sharply reminded her that a short time ago she had advocated the very opposite opinion, to which she answered: "Oh, don't be so stuffy. I don't know why you were so much against this wedding in the first place." Archie goggled; he was well aware that a husband is never right, and that no woman, including Eve, has ever been wrong; and he also acknowledged that it is a woman's privilege to change her mind, but this took the biscuit! Mercifully, at that point the 'phone rang, and Archie was saved by the bell.

Margaret grabbed it - but the call was not from New York and Gordon. It was the Laird on the line, asking for Archie to come to the phone: "For you, dear," she said seductively to her scowling mate.

"Padre," barked the Colonel, "what's this blasted helicopter doing sitting on my lawn, eh? Confounded thing nearly landed on me roses."

"Helicopter? What helicopter?" queried Archie in bewilderment.

"The one that's brought this American woman and an unfit-for-duty youth wearing one of those baseball caps. Landed here and walked right up to the front door instead of the tradesman's entrance, don't yah know. Say they are looking for you."

"Who are they and what do they want," asked Archie, after a good guess at 'who' they might be, and in what connection they would want him. Craning at his side, Margaret was all ears.

"Who are you and what do you want?" they overheard the Colonel saying. After some minutes he reported, "She says she is somebody or other's agent come to make arrangements." There was more background gabbling followed by some off stage remarks from the Colonel to his butler such as: "Can't be for the shooting, doesn't start for a bit yet, eh, Beech." Then, addressing Archie: "Better come over here at once Padre." Archie heard the butler delicately coughing in agreement.

Beech always approved everything his master did and said. When the Colonel, a member of the M.C.C., arranged his annual cricket match between an eleven from his old public school, and a conscripted scratch side from the town, his tenants, estate workers from the lands of his fellow peers, and local youths sentenced to Community Service, Beech was compelled by his master to umpire. The game was always played on St. Regulus' Day and on the links with His Lordship going in first to open the batting and be invariably clean bowled in the first over. This confronted the hapless Beech with the unwelcome sight of his revered employer puce with rage, uttering wild oaths, and brandishing his bat like a claymore. Paralyzed with fright the faithful, wrinkled, aged retainer was rendered tongue-tied, and quite incapable of uttering the word 'Out'. However, drawing heavily upon the skilful

41

diplomacy of his profession, he would solve his dilemma by lifting a finger and saying softly: "His Lordship is not in." This brilliant example of lateral thinking ensured Beech's employment for another year and, all things considered and under the circumstances, the great fish-eating Jeeves could not have done better.

His wife prodding his ribs, Archie hurriedly assured the Colonel, "I'll be right over to the House."

"Huh!" sniffed his hearer, "Cynthia's not here or she would have sent them packing…damned Yanks. Saw enough of 'em during the war."

"On my way", spluttered Archie as the line went dead and his wife helped him put on his jacket. Helicopter? Agent? What next? Well, at least that ghastly woman "Sin" wasn't there to nosey in. Five minutes later, he was at Sutor House.

CHAPTER FOUR

Veronica

The Colonel was showing a young lady round his rose garden, followed by a weedy looking, long drink of a surly youth in baggy denims, and a tee shirt lettered with the words 'Ivy League'. On closer approach and inspection, the woman, a brunette of medium height in her late twenties to early thirties, was smartly dressed in an expensively tailored skirt suit which testified to both her executive status and attractive femininity. Even Archie, who was as obtusely unobservant in these matters as most men, instantly noticed that her expensive coiffure and make up had been carefully designed to go with the sort of figure for which many a woman would kill and eat her young. This newcomer had in spades what Glasgow folk call 'cless', and everyone else calls 'charisma". Archie immediately felt that her adorable face would not only fit into, but adorn the female population of the parish. Here was a real stunner, appropriately enough, descended from heaven.

"This is...erh..." bumbled the Colonel, trying to remember whether or not the lady had told him who she was. She stuck out her delicate, gloved hand - "Veronica Winchester, how are you today?" Seeing a little further information on her credentials would not go amiss, she added with a charming smile;

"My great-grand mother was Scottish - Boston Scottish."

In contrast to the lady's impeccable attire, bearing, and polished manners, the boorish lanky Yankee teenager she had in tow stood kicking at the gravel path, moping, and making evident his lack of interest in place and persons. This caused the newly arrived Veronica to turn up the volume of her sweet voice and address him with undisguised irritation - "Duke, come over here and meet these gentlemen". Archie did not wait for a response; leaving the helicopter to take off, and the bemused looking Colonel to toddle off, he politely ushered the pair of them into his Ford Fiesta, introducing himself as he did so - "I'm the Reverend Archibald McTaggart - I believe you are looking for me."

The Lady of the Manse was rushing round tidying the house and herself when her husband's car returned. Giving guests a Highland welcome involves much smiling and many warm greetings, and Margaret supplied these in plenty as she met at the manse door the best dressed woman she had ever seen.

"Veronica, this is my wife Margaret. Margaret, this is Miss, or is it Mrs. Veronica Chester?" announced Archie. His visitor was pleasantly amused - "Win….WINchester," she tittered, "strange how over here everyone gets it wrong, it being an old English name an' all… and it's Ms., not Mrs." Stretching out her hand, she gave an enchanting smile and purred: "Such a great pleasure to meet you Margaret. Magdalene has told me so much about you I feel we are already close friends."

Margaret responded by immediately showing that Veronica's feelings about their having a close friendship were not misplaced; the two of them drew together like old school chums meeting up again after many years. Of course, as they demonstrated all the affections which go with the 'Sisterhood of Woman' each of them was also artlessly eyeing the other up as women do on first acquaintance: Margaret envied the good looks, independence, classy style of the younger woman with her interesting life of travel and high society (the Radley handbag didn't go unnoticed either); Veronica for her part envied Margaret's confidence, home, husband, family. Each woman swiftly read the other's thought processes, and moved on intuitively knowing they needed and complemented the other. In other words, having eliminated rivalry and competition, the two women took to one another right away.

So it was that this stranger, Veronica, a goddess from the skies, was introduced into the world of the Rev. & Mrs. Archibald McTaggart and came bearing that dangerous infection called "wedding fever". In the sitting room, after tea and many exchanges of pleasantries, Ms. Winchester opened her laptop and got down to business.

"Magdalene will be requiring accommodation for her guests - we estimate about two hundred prominent people, and, of course, Gordon will be inviting his friend the Prime Minister who has promised to be present if he is in the U.K. Magdalene's dear friend Sheikh bin Ryad has a castle in this part of Scotland - Is it near here?"

"Auchenshuggle Castle - not too far away, twenty five miles north, other side of the Firth," replied Archie. With raised eyebrows, he stole a sidelong glance at his wife to see if she was taking all this in, which she was indeed - in truck loads. This was big time stuff.

"No good bringing two hundred guests," Archie warned, happy to make it clear early in these discussions that he was in charge and not to be pushed around, "the kirk only holds a hundred and twenty at a squeeze."

Veronica said: "Uhm", and keyed in a memo: one hundred and twenty.

Head down, she made a mental note of Archie's caveat and moved on to the next item on her agenda: "The Sheikh will be at the wedding - do you have any personal guests you would like to invite? Magdalene is so anxious to make you feel right at the heart of everything." (How awfully nice of her, thought Archie sarcastically.) Veronica continued: "We took the liberty of looking up your family on the web, and our technical department researchers - gee! Those guys are SO clever - have listed your e-mail contacts. I see here that Rev. McTaggart's parents live in a small town called Govan, near Glasgow; and your mother, Margaret, is a wonderful woman for her age - what is she now, Eighty? well, isn't that something.....great, wonderful...says here in her C.V., let me see now... yes, here it is, she was in her young days a school teacher like yourself Margaret, and a keen member of her local Sports Club - she must have been a very busy lady. I see that since your father passed on, she now lives here with you, Margaret...Sylvia, I hope I have her name right - well, we must see that Sylvia has a special place at the wedding. I guess she is a real feisty lady. Magdalene is SO looking forwards to meeting her."

Feisty was not a word with which Mrs. McTaggart was familiar but she guessed it meant thrawn and near impossible to live with, and that was her mother all right.

"Feisty? Wait till you meet mither o' mine," Margaret said under her breath, then out loud: "Sylvia will not need a car for the wedding - she drives her own everywhere."

"Is that safe? For her I mean?" pleaded Veronica, with earnest concern.

"I don't encourage her," snapped Margaret, adding huffily, "we may live in a small country here, but have good roads called motorways." This remark puzzled Veronica for the moment for she knew there was not a motorway within thirty miles of St. Regulus, but the reproving tone of Margaret's sharp response was not wide off the mark and she intelligently resolved to go easy on bossing the McTaggart's about in their own backyard. Veronica was smart. Highly trained in salesperson skills, Veronica sensitively tinged her voice with mellowness and in tones of sympathetic understanding turned on the soft sell.

"I do hope, Margaret, that you will feel free to make any suggestions you please about the wedding - after all," she cooed, with a tinkling laugh. "It is just as much your son's wedding as ours. Please don't take it amiss if we have made some small advance preparations, but you will both appreciate that the wedding will be a major media event bringing in millions of dollars, and we must see it is done perfectly. Security will be a major problem once I leak the news in the right quarters."

Margaret and Archie listened in pained silence, at which Veronica, spotting a gap in their defences, pressed on…."Magdalene has bought The Crown Hotel, I believe it is down by the harbour, and she will be staying there the night before the wedding with, of course, her bodyguards. She can't go anywhere without them, poor girl. Did you know that President Clinton recommended The Crown for its intimate, secluded old world charm? And, of course, Magdalene will be bringing her personal chefs."

The McTaggarts did not know President Clinton had ever stayed in St. Regulus - he had visited Dornoch for the golf course, but then all the wealthy Americans did that. It was the news that The Crown had been bought by this woman Magdalene, without so much as a by your leave, which stuck in Archie's craw. The thought that some showbiz singer and dancer from Tinseltown could swoop in and buy the town pub caused Archie to almost, but not quite - his wife was present - use foul language. Instead he ground his teeth, remembered he was a minister of the Kirk, God's ordained representative in the noble and ancient borough of St. Regulus - all dues paid - and struggled to hold his tongue.

Margaret had seen Archie angry to the point of violence only twice in their long married life – once when a man with a Cockney accent kicked their car in frustration when they met, head to head, bumper to bumper on a Highland single track road. Leaping out of his Volkswagen Beetle, the cheeky chappie put his boot into Archie's offside front wheel, all the while making loud and disparaging remarks about Scotland's primitive roads, filthy weather, and financial dependence upon the misplaced generosity of the Sassenach taxpayer. Luckily for the man, Archie was wearing his clerical collar at the time, and did not take the brief confrontation beyond a hot exchange of unseemly words, which led to Archie's adversary backing down, and then backing into a lay-by. At close quarters, the sight of an angered McTaggart has alarmed many a would-be opponent into agreeing with the proverb: "Discretion is the better part of valour".

Having always considered her husband the most easy-going of men, the sight of Archie toe to toe and nose to nose with a man six inches taller than himself, with the impertinent fellow backing off, not only astonished Margaret but also filled her with pride for the female heart never beats more proudly than when discovering she has attached herself to a strong husband. The Commando in Archie was not as dormant in her man as Margaret had thought. After this incident, she did not dare issue her usual stream of backseat driving instructions, and for a whole day meekly sat in deferential silence as the man of the house drove on.

The second occasion took place years later and involved a pair of tinker thieves stealing diesel from the tank outside the manse garage. Archie, catching them in

48

the act, broke the nose of one and tied him up as the other fled. The captive was taken away by Big Jimmy, the polis, the miscreant wailing about his injuries and Civil Rights, and loudly threatening to report Archie to *his Boss* for assault. So they parted with ill-feeling and Archie pointing out to the injured party that he would have to travel up to heaven if he wished to speak to a minister's *Boss*. The police later wrote to Archie to thank him for carrying out a citizen's arrest, and assuring Margaret that her husband would not be charged with assault under European Law. Although not saying it in so many words, the letter indicated that the Chief Constable - who happened to be a second-cousin of Archie - was heavily pressing upon the prisoner the very serious inadvisability of attempting to redress his grievances by taking matters further in the hope of financial compensation.

Recalling memories of these past displays of her soul mate's wrath, Margaret sensed that all that was saving Veronica from being thrown out bag and baggage by Archie were her sex and his long-suffering Christian civility.

"More tea, dear?" smoothed Margaret, extending the teapot to her hubby, a nice try but one which did not avail to mollify Archie who was up and running, growling as he scarpered off that he was very busy and had things to do.

"Oh dear, I'm afraid I must have upset your husband," said Veronica.

"Not at all," said Margaret, "more tea?"

Glad to be left alone, the two ladies got down to arriving at a common mind, and helping each other out, as women do when it is in their interests to do so.

"You look a really homely person, Veronica - may I call you Veronica? Do you have any family yourself, back home in the United States of America?" enquired Margaret, offering a biscuit which Veronica accepted gratefully, temptation being stronger than dieting.

"Homely?" Veronica was puzzled: in the States "homely" meant everything a dedicated feminist like herself loudly denounced - dreary domesticity and the 'little woman', but she let it pass for tactical reasons. Besides, she was increasingly taking to Margaret, obviously a highly intelligent person and a real lady and Veronica met few real ladies in her line of business. It was risky, but her female intuition and hard experience told her that Margaret was worthy of her trust.

"Just my Mom in Boston, and land sakes (a folksy, 'homely' touch for effect) isn't my Mom so amazingly like your own - so feisty, such a honey. I feel SO bad at disappointing her, my Mom I mean, she SO wanted grandchildren, but Harry and I split up when I found he was unfaithful after we were engaged...at this her voice trailed off and Margaret realised with a mental jolt that Veronica was capable of being genuinely emotional. A naturally sympathetic heart is essential equipment for a *lady of the manse* so Margaret's hastened to go out to her unhappy guest

In a firm but comforting voice she stated, "It's an unfair, even cruel world at times, Veronica, men - a girl can't trust them."

"How right you are," said Veronica sadly, seconding the motion, but without explaining that her disappointment in men had been caused by a wealthy stock broker in Manhattan proving unwilling to share his life and income with her. With a shake of her lovely head she reasserted her self-belief by affirming with conviction: "I still trust in the Lord, and in Christian marriage, as I was brought up to believe by my God-fearing parents."

This sounded good to Margaret; it made her feel that she had found a friend for life in Veronica; nevertheless, the realization that the woman whose hand she was holding for comfort was as vulnerable as any other woman did not cause Margaret to lower her guard completely. A lady of the manse has to be wary at all times, and one who could out-Cynthia, the mastodon of the Woman's Guild, was not a woman to be out-witted, out-smiled, out-wept, or out-thought by a trans-Atlantic P.R. executive, even one brought up by God-fearing parents.

The mention of parents reminded Margaret to issue a warning to Veronica that in Sylvia's company it would be inadvisable to refer to her mother as a *feisty old lady*. It would equally undesirable to call her 'Sugar' or 'Honey' - Sylvia was not to be compared to sweetness, and Americanisms did not go down well with the old bat. Veronica got the message. She too had a mother whose reactions were all too often unpredictable and aggressive. Margaret now felt that she and Veronica had reached a common mind on certain important issues: firstly, keep clear of Sylvia; secondly, do not to take the McTaggarts for mugs. All that, having been made clear beyond review or question, it was with satisfaction that Margaret watched Veronica record the facts under *notebook* in her laptop.

"Veronica", began Margaret...

"Please, call me V, Veronica is so formal and I only use it with business people." Dabbing at a moist eye, she sniffed away sorrow, put on her best, well practiced smile, and for once actually meant it.

Margaret is good for me, thought Veronica. She had been having a bad time lately: Magdalene was a most irritating, infuriating employer, always pouting like a four year old, wanting everything done yesterday, forever changing her mind. Once she had completed this present job, she would be free to give that painted, insufferable egoist a large piece of her mind, topped off with a hearty *Good Riddance* - in Boston people knew how to speak their minds, yes sir, and they certainly did! Magdalene - huh! Annie O' Hara, that was her real name. Yes, she would tell the inside story when time came, and it was not long off - I'll see to it that it gets all over the tabloids how her brother Bubba shot Billy Joe O'Hare at her first wedding. Let her sue me, I'll sue HER for plenty."

The cloud which passed for a fleeting moment over her visitor's features did not pass unnoticed by her hostess; Margaret arose and scolded herself: "V, I am so sorry, I must have completely forgotten my manners - you will want to freshen up after your journey. The bathroom is at the top of the stairs."

Veronica left the room, grateful for the opportunity to dispel her bout of unhappy memories with an anti-depressant pill. Margaret, who had been wondering what Archie was up to, set off in search of him. On his study desk he had left a note to say he had gone to see the Colonel and explain about Veronica. He's making sure he heads off Cynthia, thought Margaret quite rightly. It was, as ever, her dearest wish that her nosy enemy should be kept out of the McTaggart's affairs, especially those concerning her son's marriage.

Upon Veronica's return freshly painted, the ladies conversation turned towards small talk such as the redecoration of the manse and offers from Veronica of a team of interior designers from Miami – flown over at Magdalene's expense. After grasping the notion that Veronica's offer was serious, Margaret gave the appropriate show of appreciation before politely declining the gesturer and saying: "V, do call me Maggi. That's what my close friends always call me."

It was Margaret's turn to make the running - "V, who is the young man who came with you? He seems such a nice boy?"

To hear this repulsive youth, whose companionship had been forced upon her by his equally repulsive Auntie Magdalene, to hear this repulsive, sulking, spoilt, moping youth described as *a nice boy* took some swallowing but Veronica forced it down.

"Oh, Duke, he is Magdalene's nephew, treats him like a son - eighteen last month. I see he is out in the garden with a man showing him an automobile. Duke just loves automobiles. He has four of them."

Sure enough, through the window Margaret saw Arthur enthusiastically showing his M.G. Spitfire to the aforesaid Duke who appeared so keenly interested that he was jumping around showing signs of actually being alive. Veronica took a peek - well, well, she shushed to herself ruefully; there must be life after death after all.

"That's Arthur, our younger son - Dr. Arthur. He is here acting as locum for our local doctor. She is on holiday in Jura."

"How lovely," said Vera enthusiastically, "the Jura is one of my favourite places in Eastern France. I believe the skiing is excellent there." Margaret let that one go.

Veronica tapped on her laptop: "Right, Dr. Arthur McTaggart, I see he is here down as Best Man." She peered into the screen: "He was informed of his selection by Gordon on June 1st and agreed verbally, but not in writing. I don't think there is any need at this point in time for Dr. Arthur to see the pre-nuptial agreement which will require his signature as a witness, but it is available should he wish to do so, of course."

It was at this point in time that Maggi felt the brakes should be slammed on this efficiency drive motivated by unwarranted assumptions. "V," she said in a voice filled with understanding, "I know you have your instructions to follow, but I must, in my husband's absence, tell you that he will not be conducting the wedding. In the Church of Scotland, the remarriage of a divorced person is permissible if the minister thinks the circumstances allow it, but it is most unlikely in this case seeing Magdalene's marriage has been annulled, or whatever you want to call it - we don't go in for annulments under Scots Law, see what I mean?"

Veronica was good at her job, knew this prickly problem would come up and was well prepared with an answer provided for her by her research lawyers in Harvard Law School.

"Of course, we would not dream of compromising the high principles for which Presbyterians in the States, as well as here in Scotland, are well known and respected. But you see Magdalene's annulment means she was never married in the first place. So she is a single woman and free to marry."

"Never married?" questioned Margaret, unsure whether or not to welcome this startling new information.

"You are wondering about her two children. Well, they are both adopted. Collette, she is eight, and Francis, he is nine - lovely kids."

Margaret had not been wondering at all about Magdalene's two children, their existence came as a surprising new development in this imbroglio. "What about the divorce - or rather non-divorce?" asked Margaret trying not to look flustered.

"Annulment," corrected Vera, using the voice she had perfected while selling jewellery in Macy's Department Store in New York during her less fortunate days. "The marriage was annulled." Margaret, unfamiliar with the legal term 'annulment' looked sufficiently blank for Veronica to patiently explain again.

"Magdalene was a Southern Baptist, like all her folks. For a while she was into Jewish mysticism, then spiritualism, and when she married a Roman Catholic that was when she prepared to convert into his faith. When the marriage didn't work out, the Pope personally gave the case special attention. When she speeded up the process by admitting she had been a Baptist and therefore not baptized in infancy, he agreed that she had never been married in the eyes of Holy Church and granted her 'husband' an annulment. So she is free now to marry, having been neither divorced nor married. To show her gratitude, Magdalene gave the proceeds of her major concert at the Hollywood Bowl to funding the Archbishop of Nevada's new Casino/Racecourse/Church complex on the outskirts of Vegas. His grace is considering being at the wedding and, if that is approved by Rev. McTaggart, would wish to give it his blessing. Although he cannot regard a union conducted by one of his "separated brethren" as valid, he truly regrets being unable to conduct nuptial mass for Magdalene and will give her the Church's Benediction." Margaret's grim face and forbidding silence suggested strongly to Veronica that such Jesuitical casuistry would not be received by Mr. McTaggart without strenuous objection.

"I am," of course, "simply carrying out my instructions and speaking for the Archbishop, not for myself. At times I have to say things which I personally find unacceptable." That kept Veronica's ball rolling.

She swiftly decided to withhold a second outrageous revelation, namely that Magdalenes' sister, a minister of a denomination called "The Hallelujah Latter-Day Church of the Third Coming", would like to conduct the exchange of vows - prudence required that such a proposal be put aside until the prospects of it being approved had dramatically improved. She also made a note that the Archbishop would not be welcome and to withdraw his invitation due to, she could put it to His Grace tactfully, 'due to the lack of diocesan accommodation suitable for your Eminence."

During this long afternoon, Archie had been walking his wee black mongrel bitch Pepsi round the policies of Sutor House and engaging the Colonel in precautionary discussions. The old boy seemed unable to take it in - this woman from the helicopter something to do with a wedding? Whose wedding? Some Pop Star from America, what? A secret, eh? The Laird poked at some overgrown bushes and threatened to sack his gardener for not tidying them up. They wandered on inconsequentially talking about the trout fishing, the calamitous neglect of the armed forces, and the state of the greens on the back nine until Archie ventured to say: "It won't be necessary to call a Kirk Session about this wedding business. And her Ladyship need not be troubled about it when she returns. We are keeping it on a *need to know* basis, under sealed orders, top secret, and the fewer know the better; just for now that is, of course."

"What not tell Cynthia, eh? Certainly not, Padre, the whole operation will be in jeopardy if intelligence is leaked. Walls have ears, and all that," nodded the Colonel, to whom the keeping of military secrets was the be all and end all of living. So saying, he strode off briskly leaving Archie certain that, despite the Colonel's co-operation, the story of the helicopter's arrival would be passed on to Her Ladyship by Beech as soon as she returned. This would lead to her inquisitorial questioning of her husband until he revealed all he knew. *Happily*, thought Archie, *he can't tell her much, because he knows less than I do myself about what is going on, and I know next to nothing.*

On his return, his son's car had gone from the drive, and from Veronica he learnt that Duke had gone with Arthur to see the car showrooms of Inverness. Apparently, the slobby youth had but one interest in life, and that was in car salesrooms, and Arthur was more than enthusiastic about furthering that interest. Archie was relieved – that should keep them away for the rest of the day and he made it a point to later draw to their attention the glories of the car salesrooms in Aberdeen and Perth and even further afield.

The fog of initial surprise began to clear for the McTaggarts as the day wore on. The big question was - what did Gordon have to say about all this? Could he really intend marrying this celebrity about whom they knew nothing personal except for what Veronica told them? As for Gordon, this model of Yankee 'know how' and fountain of all knowledge confessed that she had no information about where he was, what he was doing, and when he would be arriving. It was most unsatisfactory.

Still unable to reach her son in New York, Margaret decided it was time to 'phone her young friend, Katie, the young lady who ran the Post Office during the day and, in the evenings the Carnegie Library. Strategically placed to know the outgoing communications and insider gossip of the town, Katie was respected and renowned for her sealed lips, but for Margaret, who was practically her mother, Katie might well make an exception to her rules and make certain information available on the understanding it would go no further.

Single, soft spoke, a prize specimen of Scotland's bonny lassies, Katie had been right through school with Arthur, and she was virtually a member of the McTaggart clan, never out the manse, often holidaying with them. Margaret had long harboured unexpressed hopes that Katie and Gordon would one day marry: equipped with the sharp eye of a mother for match making, she had let it be known that not only did Katie come from *good stock* but was exactly the sort of wife Gordon needed to push him along and keep him on the straight and narrow. With this in mind, and knowing that Katie was clever, University educated, and like herself a well balanced Libran; Margaret completed the picture by painting in the young lady's sunny nature.

When her parents died, Katie had left - temporarily - a lucrative partnership in a law firm to take over the Post Office in St. Regulus until such time as new owners could be found, and this Margaret, with her deep-rooted Highland belief in family loyalty, found most admirable. You would not be far wrong in thinking that Katie was the daughter Margaret always wanted but never had so they were close, very close, and loving is not too strong a word for their tender relationship. Naturally they could disclose their secrets to each other with mutual confidence as occasion required.

Answering an invitation to *pop in for a chat* Katie called at the manse and following the embrace and preliminary small talk, Margaret delicately enquired if there was any news about Gordon.

To her surprise, Katie came right out with it - Gordon was rumoured to be engaged to the world's most famous and glamorous woman, namely Magdalene. This was featured prominently in all the glossy magazines. It was anything but a secret - in fact, only that day, when they met in the library, the Marquis de Mortgage had alluded to the subject while taking out a reference volume for his new book on travels in Canada.

Margaret was rocked by this disclosure; so much for the big secret. Katie showed her an expensive woman's magazine with Magdalene as the cover girl beaming a bridal smile under the headline: "Icon's Highland Wedding." Margaret ran her eye over the article inside: "Who is the lucky man?" it asked. Amongst the speculative short list of prospective candidates for Magdalene's hand there was Gordon's name - although the odds made him appear very much more of an *also ran* than a front runner. The favourite, according the magazine's gossip columnist, was a handsome Indian Maharajah worth billions of rupees who had been seen with Magdalene outside the Taj Mahal - a picture of them on page 2. However, others were tipped for the *lucky man* role, and these included the movie stars Russell Hanks, and Tom Crowe from the Hollywood stables. Whoever the unknown *lucky man* was, the race was on to find out. "Wait till Archie sees this," Margaret gasped. But Katie shrewdly noticed that whatever Archie may think, Margaret's face betrayed the fact that she was by no means averse to the publicity.

CHAPTER FIVE

The Marquis & the Mystery

The Marquis, Margaret felt certain, did not read women's glossies, so, how did he come to know about Gordon and Magdalene? Where did the Marquis come into all this? Who was he anyway? More than once she had asked Archie what was a Frenchman was doing living here, but all she got by way of an answer was, "Well, he can stay here if he likes. He writes a lot, must need the peace and quiet." Archie's typically male insouciant attitude irritated Margaret but did not dispel her suspicions.

"Something mysterious about that man," she said, nodding her head and narrowing her eyes in a knowing fashion.

The Marquis was indeed a mysterious character. He had lived on the edge of town in a modest two storey old house on Shore Street for the past three years. He was, he freely told everyone, French Canadian from the province of Quebec, a fact to which Mr. McTaggart could testify because he had, in his own younger days, spent a year there as student assistant to a Canadian minister whom he had met when they shared digs during their time together at theological college in Edinburgh.

Archie had unpleasant memories of Quebec: his 'bishop' served a congregation of Scots ex-pats in a copper mining town in Upper Quebec Province and the mine owner not only owned the mine, but with it the town. The guy was a despot who ruled over his little kingdom unchallenged: at every election he was elected mayor by dint of threats that he would dig up the main street if the constituents did not vote for him. The hospital was his too, and creditably equipped (in case he or his family needed it), but as nobody wished to live and work in the remote backwoods of northern Canada the place was staffed by nuns who possessed great motivation but only a minimal knowledge of nursing and medicine. The chances of a seriously ill person surviving a stay in the hospital were therefore slight but this did not trouble the good Sisters of Notre Dame for they saw their primary task being to arrange for the safe passage into heaven of the souls of their patients detouring them from hell via the Last Rites received from those authorised to bind and loose.

Archie's *bishop* was an amiable, lumberjack-size fellow who spent a good deal of his time sleeping – there being not much else to do in that neck of the woods. When one day he was badly crushed in his car by a falling tree Archie, who narrowly escaped injury himself, managed to stop a passing truck and rush the poor guy to hospital. There the sisters flapped around clucking helplessly and telling the distraught Archie that they had no blood of the type needed for a transfusion to save the accident victim's life. Very fortunately, Archie realised that he had the right blood type handily on tap in his own veins and immediately offered to donate the necessary amount. The nuns told him to lie down, a needle was inserted, and he was told to pump his arm up and down. The result was not a flow of red and white corpuscles into a container, but Archie's blood pressure shooting up to red alert, the needle shooting out, and his blood splattering the ceiling. The Mother Superior turned out to see the spectacle, and to issue effusive apologies in a French accent peculiar to the region. Archie, not being in a receptive mood and finding her brand of French unintelligible, mistakenly thought he was being given a telling off and responded with some hot words in English which the good lady fortunately did not understand.

"They damned near killed me," swore an irate Archie, who insisted on doing the business again, but this time under the supervision of a doctor. Happily the blood saved his boss' life, and the nuns had to put their patient's soul on hold until another day. It was said that if an emergency arose during the Second World War which threatened the life of the Pope he would be evacuated to the safety of French-speaking, medieval Quebec—a fate Archie earnestly prayed would never befall any man.

The Marquis de Mortgage, if that was his real name, certainly knew his Upper Quebec and shared Archie's distaste for its attractions. Archie liked the guy. Stimulating intellectual conversation was not in plentiful supply amongst his parishioners, and, finding the Marquis agreeable, knowledgeable, respectful, and welcoming, Archie paid him regular visits. Always interested in well-informed, amusing people, Archie took especial pleasure in discussing the Marquis's books - his latest called 'Travels in Israel' had led to the bet of £10 that Archie could not swim in the Sea of Galilee and the Firth on the same day - a bet he had won on returning from the Holy Land. Despite the Marquis' ambivalent attitude towards Christianity and non-attendance at Sunday worship Archie, always given to taking people as he found them, got on well with this companionable acquaintance whose wit and ability to write he admired.

The Marquis was a radio ham and the attic of his house was crammed with sophisticated, expensive equipment. He would take Archie up there for a chat with all sorts of people in far away place like The Falklands - where Archie had come to know other radio hams from his wartime service there. Talking to somebody in Tokyo or Rio or Manila or some other exotic place opened the world to Archie and brought him so much enjoyment that he was forever popping in on the Marquis. It was more fun than the internet because you could talk to people directly. For the Marquis the radio was not a hobby but an essential and secure part of his business: it kept him linked to the film and entertainment industries over in The States on whose behalf he worked as a playwright and script writer. At a presentation in Hollywood for an award for screen writing a highly successful comedy series set in New Orleans, he was asked how he, living in the isolation of the North of Scotland, could have written so descriptively about a city he had never seen. His answer was:

"Well, I guess if you live in a place like St. Regulus, you need a vivid imagination." Archie loved that line—he chuckled over it often, and would say to his folks with a grin when they moaned about St. Regulus: "Well, you need a vivid imagination to live here, you know!"

Pressed to estimate the age of the Marquis, Archie would have guessed mid-thirties to forty. A very handsome man, who caught the eye of every female in St. Regulus, he lived alone and kept to himself, but was invariably charming when encountered on one of his visits to the grocery shop, or Post Office. Katie saw a good deal of him as he was constantly sending and receiving letters and parcels from California. With a nod and a wink, he had told her about Magdalene's future wedding to a future Prime Minister of Great Britain, at a time when such a bombshell was being only vaguely rumoured in the transatlantic media. Katie knew that American insider intelligence on such matters was often little more than wild speculation compared to our slightly more sober reporting on this side of the pond, so she didn't take the Marquis at all seriously. Yet, at the same time he had left her feeling uncomfortably curious; he seemed strangely keen to tell her about Magdalene and Gordon—how was he so sure that the *lucky man* was Gordon and not one of the other several contenders? Maybe he was trying to impress her? Flirting? Chatting her up? Katie was too good looking for a Frenchman to resist her attractions - she didn't need her female intuition to tell her that, it was obvious. She would ask him more about Gordon at the right opportunity; like all lady-killers, the Marquis could be easily taken in by a clever woman, and she would find out how and what he knew.

As they sipped tea in the manse kitchen Katie was very surprised to discover that Margaret regarded the rumour of a possible wedding between Magdalene and Gordon as some sort of big secret. The news that it was in the glossies had visibly shaken Margaret. Who had told Margaret, and presumably Mr. McTaggart, to keep it a secret? Must have been Gordon - what was he playing at?

While Katie ran her mind over these questions, Margaret sat before her feeling very foolish - the whole world knew about the wedding, certainly not in detail but in enough outlines to start further probing. Set free of her irrelevant obligation to keep a burst secret, Margaret felt able to enlighten her trusted young friend completely and tell her all she knew. This she did, in a hushed voice, though her listener could not understand why she was whispering if the secret was already out. It must be on the T.V. news by now.

Amongst the many features of Katie's character which Margaret esteemed was her gift for composure, but even so, when told that Gordon really was about to marry Magdalene and that it was not media guesswork, and furthermore that the wedding was to be right here in St. Regulus, Margaret was taken aback to see with what cool detachment Katie received the momentous news. She had assumed that Katie would have been not a little upset, taking it all very personally as a severe blow to her own marriage prospects with regard to sharing a double-bed with Gordon as Mrs. G. McTaggart. Plainly, Katie's nose was not one bit put out - she was not in the least disappointed to hear that Gordon was about to hitch up with another woman; indeed, it was not Katie but Margaret who had to do the readjusting, realising that her long cherished maternal hopes of a dream union of Katie and Gordon had been very wide of the mark. The idea that Margaret entertained thoughts of her marrying Gordon had not entered Katie's head.

Placing a consoling arm around on her companion with a tenderness born of Sunday School memories of the story of Ruth and Naomi, Margaret walked Katie home in a strange, sympathetic silence, which left her young companion wondering what was on Margaret's mind. It was only after they had parted that the penny dropped: "Good heavens!" exclaimed Katie, startling herself, "Margaret thought I was hoping to marry Gordon...did he tell his mother we were getting engaged or something?" It gave her a funny feeling that first with the Marquis and now with Margaret there was more going on here than met the eye.

Returning to the manse, having learnt from Katie a great deal she did not know about Magdalene's fame and career, Mrs. McTaggart's earlier uncertainty about the prospect of her elder son marrying such a woman began to return, leaving her pondering what her attitude should be. However, one thing had become quite clear: Katie had never entertained any thought of marrying Gordon that was for sure from her reaction to the news of his engagement. Most disappointing, but a mother's optimism when it comes to match making never dies, and the thought vaguely crossed Margaret's mind that Arthur might…well, he needed the steadying influence of a good wife, and Margaret dreaded he might leap into some calamitous romance with a stranger whom she had not had the opportunity to vet.

Her thoughts churning like a tumble drier, she found the manse was unoccupied, empty, and lonely; Archie had gone to a funeral; David, back from his jaunt with the obnoxious Duke, had gone to his first surgery. Veronica's luggage was gone, and she with it. A note, written in a fine hand on scented paper, was propped up on the mantelpiece…..

"Dear Maggi,

I have just received an invitation from her Ladyship at Sutor House for Duke and I to stay there until the wedding ceremony is concluded. It may be a suitable place for Magdalene's retinue too, if an arrangement to that effect can be concluded.

The House is roomy inside and grand outside as I saw when I flew in, so it will be eminently suitable for photography. I am sure you will approve, and it pleases me to think that I will not be imposing upon your hospitality by asking for my personal accommodation in your home. I thank you for your company and wise counsel and hope to benefit further from our friendship in the coming days.

Affectionately, V."

Margaret dropped herself into an armchair and let the letter drop to the floor. She was certainly relieved that this Veronica who had barged into her ordered existence was not intending to put up at the manse, but highly troubled and displeased that her great enemy had nipped in and cornered the market in wedding arrangements. It was HER son who was getting married – what was that interfering Cynthia woman doing shoving her nose into HER family matters. Margaret was so angry that she wrote a letter on her best notepaper in carefully crafted copperplate handwriting saying...

"Dear V,

I quite understand your acceptance of Cynthia's kind invitation–she wrote 'Cynthia' pretty sure Veronica would call her that, following the American penchant for the sort of familiarity her Ladyship hated – *it is very good of her ladyship to provide you with accommodation, especially as she suffers from poor health and rarely entertains guests. Cynthia puts on a brave face and never refers to her mental and physical disabilities, so please do not make any mention of them.*

You can have every assurance that Mr. McTaggart and I will keep your confidences private as we are sure you will keep ours. Hope we can meet very soon,

Most sincerely, Maggi."

She sealed the letter feeling much better, and gave some boys playing in the woods a pound to run round and deliver it to Sutor House.

CHAPTER SIX

The Turning Point

The appearance on the streets of the town of two young men wearing full Highland dress and addressing passers-by, in American accents, with the friendly greeting, "How are you today?" aroused general comment. It had been many years since missionary Mormons from Salt Lake City had given up hopes of ever making converts on the doorsteps of *Reggie*, so, if not Mormons, who were these crew-cut all-American boys who in height and muscularity, if not in pigmentation, resembled O. J. Simpson? Judging from their attire, they seemed to be under the impression that every male in Scotland outfitted himself with a kilt, silver buttoned jacket, frilled cuffs, and dirk, and that by similarly kitting themselves out, they were blending unobtrusively into the picturesque sort of community they had seen portrayed in *Brigadoon*. They certainly showed great interest in every part of the town, photographing it from all angles and making notes. They had been observed emerging from the Crown Hotel and thither they eventually returned.

That the last guests had gone, and that the bar side of the hotel was about to close was of considerable interest in a town which depended on the tourist trade. The story was that the owner of the Crown and his female 'partner' had concluded their sexual relationship by his leaving her and going off with the barmaid. This story was misleading and incorrect, the truth being that it was not the landlord who had gone off with the barmaid but his former *partner*.

"I thought she was one of them," commented an elderly lady who had been a W.A.A.F. during the Second World War. "When I joined up I was so naive that I thought some of the girls were just extraordinarily affectionate until I heard the word lesbian for the first time and they tried it on with me. They didn't get me into bed with them, I can tell you!"

So the venerable borough of St. Regulus realised it had harboured and lost its first known lesbian - any previous ones would have been quickly spotted and the talk of such a wee place. Meantime, the barmaid's mother, making a virtue of necessity, let it be known publicly that, in her opinion, her daughter was unashamedly defying outmoded convention and demonstrating that old fashioned morality was a thing of the past - and a good thing too! Privately, however, she informed her highly embarrassed sisters that she would kill that perverted old bitch at The Crown for seducing her innocent, childlike daughter, and taking her off to God knows where. If she ever laid hands on her...etc., etc...

Doubtless relieved to be rid of his former partner in business and bed, the former owner of the hotel speedily bought the town's only other public house, which had been closed for several years, and let it be widely known that he intended refurbishing it, no expense spared. He moved in, taking with him a new 'sleeping partner' to housekeep and mind the bar: a well preserved widow lady of his own age, with a shady reputation, who was there, everyone knew, to pull more than pints for him.

It was obvious that The Crown had been sold to some Americans, for a very great sum, but the question remained - who were they and what were they doing in "Reggie"? Who exactly had bought and paid for it, and why? Speculation was rife, but the former owner gave nothing away about the mysterious eccentric Yanks in occupation. Whoever was behind all this, what could they want with The Crown and its genteel summer regular clientele, and its crusty old winter evening barflies?

Presumably, it would reopen in due course - but then, maybe not. Street conversation fair buzzed.

The town had not been so agog with excitement since the fleet anchored in battleship row in the Firth and sailors flooded the streets on Saturday nights filling the pubs, dancing in the Gladstone Hall, and packing out the pictures at the British Legion. Something was definitely afoot - the helicopter at Sutor House, the business of the hotel, the appearance of a young guy in a baseball cap driving a Rolls Royce containing an expensively dressed businesswoman about the place, the distracted looks of the minister and his normally placid wife... And then there was the press sniffing about, phoning the Provost, Bill Ross, and his brother Fraser the chemist, for what they vaguely called 'any news'.

The bowling club, the information centre of 'Reggie', was humming with gossip that what lay behind all this activity was that the Laird had struck it rich with oil: drilling of a geyser in his walled market garden, it was said, was yielding a fountain of black gold. In previous years, an unscrupulous international financier, equipped with insider knowledge of the money markets, had put one over on the Laird's geriatric family Solicitor by buying up the estate's shoreline dirt cheap before the discovery of North Sea oil and gas became public knowledge. The Laird had been done out of millions and all honest men agreed that he been unjustly left in impecunious circumstances. Sympathy for their chieftain was considerably strengthened by the failure of the said Sassenach plutocrat to honour his promises to benefit the citizens through a Town Development Fund which never materialized. Therefore, the spreading belief that the Laird had hit the jackpot, and in his own backyard at that, was widely and warmly welcomed until the rumour reached the ears of McEwan the gardener. That normally uncommunicative man scotched the tale by letting it be known that the drilling was for a spring water fountain to supply an ornamental pond in honour of Lady Cynthia's seventieth birthday. The geyser which had shot high in the sky was not petroleum, just H^2O. Whatever the reason for all this American activity in town, it was not due to oil. What was going on? What did these gum chewers want in 'Reggie'?

Archie had been unusually grumpy that afternoon while conducting the funeral of old Donald who had dropped down dead in the nursing home when told he had won a thousand pounds in the National Lottery. Anticipating mortality, he had arranged for his body to go to medical research; when his Solicitor had asked why he was so determined about this, Donnie had stated emphatically that the only way he could stop his detestable next door neighbour going to his funeral was not to have one at all. However, the best laid schemes being what they are for mice and men, nobody collected the old boy's remains, so Archie proceeded to bury him in the traditional 'Reggie' manner.

Wearing his black funeral kilt - "It doesn't show the dirt", explained Archie, the minister, followed by a column of solemnly shuffling along men folk, duly delivered the boxed Donnie to the graveyard beside the kirk, and there the old boy cashed in his six score years and ten and joined his forefathers. For once, Dr. McTaggart was not responsible in this case for helping the Grim Reaper to harvest a citizen of St. Regulus, for which small mercy Arthur's father gave thanks.

A chill wind made the silent mourners shiver as they proceeded to leave the cemetery, at which point Archie said brightly: "Any of you boys like a drink to warm you up?" Eyes lifted, ears pricked up, heads nodded in the

71

affirmative, a chorus of grateful 'Ayes' followed. "Well, boys", said the caretaker of their souls, "look into that grave - that's where drink put Donnie, and that's where it will take you!" So saying he wheeled and stumped off leaving them asking what was up with Erchie, for he was well known to be no teetotaller.

His mood was no better when he got home and Margaret said to him: "How did you get on at the funeral?" Receiving no reply she continued: "I don't know why you took it; Donnie told everybody he was an atheist."

"Atheist," answered her hubby loftily, "aye he WAS an atheist, but (the Glaswegian in him coming out) he's no wan noo." She left it at that.

"Two crazy Americans wandering round the town in kilts," said Archie as he took off his black shoes and put on his comfy 'bauchles'. "Where is Veronica what'sit?"

He got the whole story as she made scrambled eggs for a late supper. One thing Margaret loved about her husband was that he never complained about anything she put on the table; at the same time it irked her that he was so compliant that she sometimes had to provoke him to complain. Saving a husband from laziness - which he confuses with happy contentment - is a wifely duty not to be neglected; he has to be stung, prodded from time to time for his own good. So, as Margaret shovelled the eggs on his plate, she testily snapped: "Well, what are you going to do about it?"

If there was one thing Archie had learnt during his thirty years of married life it was never to weaken on these occasions but to instantly counter-attack - a tactic he had learnt from his dear wife who regularly employed it to great effect.

"What am I going to do about what?" he retorted sharply. "I'm not doing this blasted wedding if that's what you mean. I'm not doing it, that's what I'm going to do about it, no way, and when I get my hands on that boy I'll choke him. Has Mr. Bloody High and Mighty Gordon 'phoned yet?"

"Don't swear," said Margaret testily. Her reply to his question being in the negative, they ate in silence awhile until Margaret said with distaste, "V and that boy with her have gone to stay at Sutor House - Cynthia invited them." She passed Veronica's written message over to him.

"God knows what the Laird will say about having a tribe of pot smoking, tobacco chewing, moonshine swilling mountain men coming to stay under his roof. I wish to God he would have the guts sometime to sort Cynthia out once and for all...that confounded woman!"

They cleared the table and then sat by the unlit fire in irritable mood sipping their tea. Archie flipped through the newspaper in a distracted fashion until Margaret, having had one of the most stressful days in her life, cleared off for her read in her bath before bed. This left Archie to pack up his kit, wash his socks, and set out tomorrow's clean underclothes as a good Marine always does and always will. He watched a late night film on T.V. until far too late, yawned, lost interest, switched off and crept quietly upstairs. As he did so he heard the clock striking one o'clock and Arthur coming in banging doors and whistling merrily. He's late back and mighty happy about something, thought his tired father as he slipped into bed and immediately fell asleep.

Archie, as his training for the coveted and strenuous 'green beret' had drummed into him, was up early. He no longer ran two miles before breakfast instead he walked a mile briskly as his age required. On returning, he read the Bible lesson for the day from the lectionary, and proceeded into his morning prayers during which he particularly drew the Lord's attention to the matrimonial intentions of his elder son, and his own need for guidance on the perplexing issues these were raising for himself, his wife, the town, and, indeed, the world at large.

It was his habit to have porridge followed by a boiled egg for breakfast. For years he had timed the boiling of his egg by singing, *sotto voce*, the stirring hymn 'Onward Christian Soldiers', the verses of which (by Sabine Baring Gould) will, when sung to the tune St. Gertrude (by Sir Arthur Seymour Sullivan), last precisely five minutes. While waiting for his egg to be timed the specified number of minutes, Archie invariably attempted to fill in the previous day's "Press & Journal" crossword, counting himself happy if he could answer any of the clues, for he had absolutely no aptitude for such puzzles though unwilling to admit it. When Archie resolved to keep at a task he kept at it, as a Christian soldier should, for he was not, as he said of himself somewhat boastfully, an 'if and but' man.

This determination was one of the endearing qualities possessed by her husband which attracted his wife. She saw her husband as a man who knew where he was going in life and why. Unlike most people she knew, Archie was a man completely contented to be himself as God had made him and this gave him his easy-going, laid-back style. Non-competitive, Archie treated everyone the same friendly way. He was insatiably curious and interested in everyone and everything, tolerant of others and their *point de vue*, yielding easily to persuasion and entreaty. This bookish, absent-minded, idealistic bedfellow of hers could, however, at times turn unexpectedly stubborn and obstinate and it surprised people who thought they knew him well to discover that on certain issues he would not budge once his mind was made up.

Margaret, like all women, regarded it as her natural prerogative to change her mind as frequently as required. This facility comes in very handy when needed but it makes it impossible for the female mind to understand the male psyche. Archie's withdrawals into silence, fear of intrusion into his thoughts, obsessive focus on plans and schemes, all such mysterious activities Margaret had learnt to tolerate - up to a point - but not to comprehend. But that mattered little; female intuition was what counted, and Margaret's intuition infallibly guided her into subtle and effective ways of getting a husband to change his mind without him realising why.

Such was the situation in the days following the arrival of Gordon's astonishing message followed by Veronica's appearance from out the air. While Archie had been hardening his heart, Margaret had been increasingly softening hers to the benefits of proceeding to this proposed wedding. She had already approved the pros and eliminated the cons and was now at the stage of lying in bed at nights dreaming of the joys of family weddings: visions of the bridegroom's proud mother, the centre of attention, entering the kirk in a perfectly fitting cream outfit with matching large hat; sweet dreams of famous guests laughing and videoing and clapping as Magdalene, the icon, kisses her new mother-in-law; reveries of world-wide television coverage swam into her shut eye fantasy…here, at last, a long overdue opportunity to let the unthinking know that she, Margaret McTaggart, was not a frowsy nobody from the sticks, not 'just' the minister's wife: no! it was high time people knew that she had had a life before St. Regulus and was a sophisticated lady experienced in foreign travel, someone behind whose name lined up a queue of University degrees. The author of several highly regarded books and lectures on education,

Margaret had been described in her younger days by one reviewer as 'a rising star' in the teaching profession. In short, Margaret was fed up being treated as if she had 'come up the Clyde in a banana boat - a term she picked up from Archie which summed up her feelings very well.

The more she dreamed the more attractive grew the benefits accruing from going ahead with the wedding: from an unselfish point of view, there would be the business and world wide attention brought to the town, not forgetting the money badly needed to repair the roof of the kirk. She imagined vividly Prime Minister Gordon ceremonially dedicating the refurbished church, and then opening a newly built church hall paid for by Magdalene's millions. The thought that Lady Cynthia would be green with jealousy added immensely to Margaret's pleasure and enthusiasm for a wedding which would be the envy of Westminster Abbey and that snobby Church of England with their monopoly of state occasions. Why, Princess Anne would certainly want to come, and might even bring the Queen with her from Balmoral.

Margaret was fond of her bed and not easily aroused, but she forsook her usual breakfast appearance in curlers and dressing gown to show up bright and smart at table. Her bouncy entrance did not escape Archie's notice and right away he said to himself:

"She wants me to change my mind about taking the wedding."

"I've been thinking," she eventually said, in that change of voice which Archie had long since learnt warned him he was about to be enticed like Adam into some major indiscretion, "I've been thinking we owe it to our son to conduct his wedding"

We? thought Archie. *It's me, I'm the one doing the wedding.* But he let it go.

"He would never forgive us," she went on, "if we turned against him and let him down. Don't you think we MUST make allowances dear, and stand by him, I'd never forgive myself (she meant Archie) if we said no. Anyway, he's asked Arthur to be best man. At least talk it over with Veronica - Magdalene was widowed soon after her first marriage while very, very young, poor lassie, and her second was annulled, so she was not married at all in that case. Veronica will explain it all to you, and there must be proof available for you to check if you insist."

"We've been through this before," said Archie, "at one time you were dead against it."

"Not at all; I was just considering. You never listen to what I say."

A husband of experience is familiar with accusations of selective deafness and he can deal with them, but Margaret's tergiversation over this wedding was mind-blowing.

All Archie could lamely say was: "What is she? A Roman Catholic? A Bible Belt Baptist? She might be a Hindu for all I know." Sulkily raising the cup of coffee Margaret had so thoughtfully served him to his mouth, he burnt his tongue and spluttered:

"My God, Margaret, why didn't you tell me this was scalding hot?" The unintentional diversion came at the right moment to catch Archie off guard.

"So, that's settled then; tell Veronica. But tell her we need to know what is going on. She is such a sensible person. Talk to her."

"Sensible - how do you know she is sensible? You only met the woman a couple of days ago."

His protests were too little too late. Margaret brought him his coat. "We need milk, dear, bring some in when you come back," she called to him as he set off for

Sutor House, determined to wrap things up once and for all. He was really fed up with this unwarranted intrusion into his routine and his plans, and he was resolved that nothing was going to interfere with his playing in the Church of Scotland versus Church of England annual golf match in a fortnight's time. A man can only put with so much from a wife who has no idea what is important in life.

Walking Pepsi up the drive to the mansion, he encountered the Laird walking towards him surrounded by his spaniels. The dogs sniffed and the Colonel puffed: "Ah, Padre, just on my way to see you. Must talk about this Veronica filly. The memsahib has been talking to her for hours in the morning room. Something to do with another female called Maudlin—must be named after my old Oxford College, can't think why. Who is she?"

"A rock and roll star from Hollywood," replied Archie, wrinkling his nose.

"Another American, eh?" mused the Colonel, forgetting Archie had just told him this. "Some sort of public entertainer, I suppose?"

"I wouldn't be surprised," replied Archie sourly, "there's an endless supply of them; all rich as Croesus."

"The bounder wants to buy Sutor House, and if I won't sell wants to rent it for a month. Offering two million for the house and half a million for a rental, don't you know?"

The Laird's screwed up countenance showed that he was deeply impressed by the sums mentioned. Archie was no less impressed for this was indeed remarkable information - on the table millions for Sutor House! They stopped walking: "Pounds or dollars?" asked an astonished Archie.

"Forgot to ask. Expect the old girl will sort that out with Ver…what's her name."

Archie was not listening - this unexpected new development required considerable thought: he had come to see Veronica to tell her in no uncertain terms that in spite of his wife's dreams and urgings, there would be no wedding and to forget it and go back whence she came. He had steeled himself to do this for going against Margaret's wishes invited unpleasant repercussions and, more importantly, involved disregarding his own guilty fears that he was foolishly throwing away the chance of a lifetime to re-roof the kirk. His resolve, which admittedly had been faltering, now collapsed under the impact of the Colonel's astounding information.

A walk up the long driveway to the Big House told the story of why the Laird needed money and needed it badly; the lodge house at the ornamental gates was closed up and the gates were rusted open; the road was potholed; the rotted wooden bridge over the burn a dangerous hazard to pedestrians and light traffic alike. Archie knew that the Colonel nowadays employed only Hector the gamekeeper, and old McEwan the gardener, and these stalwarts worked more out of loyalty than for financial remuneration.

Eighteenth century Sutor House was no Chatsworth, nor Blenheim, but it was an imposing architectural gem, opulent and well appointed; if Jane Austin had had an opportunity to visit the Colonel's stately home she would doubtless have written a novel about it. But alas! dry rot, that cancer of fine aged buildings, was these days in evidence in the less frequented parts of the building and the funds to eradicate it unavailable. In short, the Laird was 'skint' though too proud to admit it to himself. He left Her Ladyship to face the facts, factor the estate, and pay the bills, knowing only too well that money and time and the family silver were running out.

The Laird, a latter-day Mr. Micawber, had little financial acumen, and behind him ran a trail of failed business ventures: there had been the battery chickens, the pig rearing, and the market gardening - all costly disasters. Veronica's practiced eye and her diligent researches into how things stood with the finances of Sutor House told her that Her Ladyship would jump at the chance to do the *noblesse oblige* act and take any dough which might be forthcoming. Cynthia's oblique approach to negotiations over Magdalene's offer smoothed the deal to a satisfactory, face saving conclusion as both parties knew it would. The House would be rented. What Magdalene wanted Cynthia also wanted - trebles all round! The noble old pile would be saved, hallelujah!

It was now crystal clear to Archie that what she wanted in the way of a wedding Magdalene was also going to get. No way could he deny the Laird salvation from bankruptcy; he could make a fortune by accepting temporary renting for a few short weeks. The last thing "Reggie" folk wanted to see was the Laird being compelled to sell out to some foreigner from Russia or Arabia, or some other undesirable place.

"If you rent out for a month," asked Archie, "I take it you'll stay in residence until they've gone." This was not the sort of thing one says to a man whose ancestors built Sutor House on the site of the ruined 12th century Sutor Castle.

In bygone centuries the Laird's clansmen forefathers had defended the stronghold's battlements against the likes of the dreaded Wolf of Badenoch; amused themselves by hanging marauding MacKenzies from its turrets (after torture as and when required); and, most notably, the McSutor clansmen had fought for Bruce at Bannockburn. The notorious 'Black Sutor', Chief of Clan McSutor, never forgave the Campbells for massacring the Macdonald's of Glen Coe, not because the McSutors liked the Macdonald's any better than did the Campbells, but because they considered it to be their honour to have first choice of all massacring as guaranteed by Royal Charter granted by William the lion.

"Stay on? Damn me, Padre, I'm not moving out of my own house for anybody," exploded the monarch of a good deal of what he surveyed from the windows of Sutor House, "these people can stay in the servants' quarters."

Archie considered this expression of indignation well merited, but realized fully that the offer of servants' accommodation was unlikely to find acceptance by the incoming mega bucks paying super-star and the Colonel would have to reconsider in due course.

They proceeded up the grand stone staircase leading up to the entrance to the House, and were met there by Beech who stood at attention before his master looking as stiff, and still as a grandfather clock. From this dignified retainer in his claw hammer jacket they learnt that Her Ladyship had left for Inverness airport where she was taking a flight to London and the Kensington offices of the family solicitors: Hook, Line, & Sinker. Also absent was the 'American lady' who had been, he reported, driven away in the car belonging to the Marquis gentleman from the Shore Road in the town. He did not know their destination or when they would return.

Absent-mindedly the old war horse trotted indoors followed at a respectful distance by his butler; "Bless my soul! Gawn to London, eh?" muttered His Lordship shaking his head and forgetting to bid his pastor farewell.

Archie jogged round to the residence of the Marquis *tout suite,* mystified as to why Veronica had gone off with him. Did they know each other? They must do; so then why had she not mentioned the Marquis to him before? He was sure she had not mentioned knowing the Marquis to Margaret. Something unexplained, suspicious even, was going on: how could Veronica and the Marquis possibly know each other? Och, there was no way they could possibly be meeting here in St. Regulus by chance. So, what were they up to? Where were they going together? Archie intended to find out.

CHAPTER SEVEN

Wedding Fever

On his way along the shore road Archie strolled past the lighthouse on the rocky point protruding from the harbour out into the Firth. A 60ft. high, stubby Victorian structure, built by the uncle of Robert Louis Stevenson, stood bleached white by the summer sunshine. There he met 'Daft Willie', an eccentric local worthy who was as much a part of "Reggie" as the lighthouse itself, and a man greatly respected by the minister and the community.

Willie was wearing on his gigantic, cadaverous frame as odd an assortment of garments as jumble sales can furnish, and on his head a personally designed helmet of cardboard topped by one of those plastic whirligigs popular with small children at fairgrounds. As Willie wandered the town at all hours in all weathers, day in day out, he was as familiar a sight as the seagulls and, though tourists sneakily sniggered at his appearance, Willie's neighbours knew that he was not as daft as his dress sense and nickname suggested.

In his youth, during the war, 'Daft Willie' had served in the Observer Corps, his post a fort set high on the heavily fortified South Brae which bristled with guns guarding the narrow entrance to the Firth and the warships safely anchored therein. From his concrete eerie, Willie could diligently sweep far out to sea with powerful binoculars, ever on the lookout for U-boats or Luftwaffe raiders speeding in from Norway.

It was during those long, lonely hours of vigil that he logged and reported on weather conditions, and when peace robbed him of this important and enjoyable duty, Willie continued to record the weather conditions as a matter of habit. Ever scanning the skies on his interminable walks round and round the town, covering the walls of the bothy he called home with charts and graphs, Willie would readily supply any enquirers he met on his travels with astonishingly accurate weather forecasts. The residents of "Reggie" were thus the best informed people in the world when it came to meteorology, for which they were grateful to "Daft Willie", their resident human barometer. The Observer Corps badge proudly displayed on his lapel, and the whirligig wind-direction finder on his head, showed that Willie meant serious business on the weather front; where the B.B.C. forecasts often erred, Willie's never did.

The only time Willie was not out touring the streets was when he was ringing the bell of the kirk on a Sunday morning – a responsibility he took most religiously, and with such immaculate timing that the townsfolk set their clocks by Willie's bell. It was his disconcerting practice to stop passers-by in the street, friend and stranger, and correct the accuracy of their watches by his own turnip-sized pocket timepiece - Willie's physique, strange attire, and 'strong language' advertised the wisdom of co-operation.

If Willie had any flaw to his generous nature - and he did - it was an inclination to speak his mind in language which would have made a Sergeant in the Scots Guards blush. On Sundays, worshippers who had been absent for several Sundays could expect to be greeted with an earful of reproach from the bell-ringer in the porch: "Where the...hell have you been," or words to that effect. The tolerance of the members of the congregation was often stretched by Willie's fruity forthrightness but it never snapped, doubtlessly because the doorkeeper of the House of the Lord knew too much about everybody in the town.

Never wrong about the weather, Willie was also never wrong about people; he had everyone summed up, and did not hesitate to say what he thought of people he disliked. This was an embarrassment to Archie but he knew there was nothing to be done about it, and he valued Willie's worth when it came to accurately assessing individuals because Archie, a poor judge of character, was inclined to think the best of others and sometimes lived to regret it. Nothing happened in "Reggie" but Willie, the trained spotter, knew about it. Archie's loyal, peripatetic spy constantly supplied him with information for which his boss was most grateful, the parish minister always being the last person to be told what is going on.

Willie had an uncanny way of reading Archie's mind; "If you're looking for thon French loon he's gaed awa wi' thon Yankee wumman in a speedboat. Half an hoor ago. Be hauf way across the Firth by noo." So saying, and having no further knowledge to impart on the subject. Willie leapt onto an invisible bicycle, and rode off without additional conversation. Archie checked his watch.

Speedboat? The Marquis didn't have a speedboat, or any other kind of boat. Never seen him out sailing – where was he taking Veronica? When were they coming back? He was getting really fed up with these mysterious goings on; why did nobody ever tell *HIM* anything?

With the Marquis gone, Archie called in at the surgery which was closed for lunch. There he surprised Arthur and Katie in very intimate conversation, *tête-a-tête* stuff. Somewhat embarrassed at what looked like an assignation a flustered Katie muttered to Archie something about collecting a prescription, and Archie muttered to Katie something about returning a library book, while Arthur fiddled with his stethoscope.

After a lull in this brief conversation, Katie said: "Veronica asked me to let you know she will 'phone you this evening. The Marquis has taken her to Auchenshuggle Castle to check that the Sheikh knows that Magdalene will be spending her honeymoon night at Sutor House and not at the castle - distance, security, and that sort of thing. And she says to tell you that Duke has flown down to Earls' Court for the motor-show and will not be coming back until the wedding day." It was pretty clear to Archie that his younger son wanted him to promptly withdraw his intrusive presence and shove off, which he did.

They seem pretty chummy, he mused. *I must tell Margaret; Arthur and Katie, eh? Well, well.* He felt quite cheered up.

It is not possible for a parish minister as well liked as Erchie to walk along Bank Street, or Church Street, the two principal thoroughfares of St. Regulus without having his progress halted every few yards. So it was that on his way home, Mr. McTaggart was repeatedly stopped to receive the latest news of his parishioner's ailments and cures.

Auld Lizzie (byname "Christmas" because she was always wailing 'No well, No well") arrested his progress to say: "Oh, meenister, I've got stones."

Archie sympathised: "Sorry to hear it, Lizzie. Are you seeing a specialist?"

The Auld Yin straightened and cheered up: "Och yes, Mr McTaggart, I'm tae see a geologist."

Archie nodded in confirmation: "A geologist - well that's the very fella to see for stones right enough, Lizzie."

He met Madge, as she was hirpling along the street. A lady dedicated to being fit and slim, Madge spent her days running marathons in far off places. She was thin; Archie used to say that she was so thin that her skeleton was on the outside and not the inside of her body. Madge's conversation disclosed that she had an infected ankle. "Will you have to cancel your Himalayan marathon?" Archie asked in a pained voice.

"No, no, not at all," she replied brightly, "Dr. Arthur has given me some anti-bionic tablets." *Bionic Wonder Woman Madge? now there's a thought,* mused Archie, trying to keep a straight face.

When not being told of forthcoming operations, it is a clergyman's fate to listen to lengthy reports about the doings of nephews and nieces in faraway places like New Zealand while stifling a yawn and pretending to show some interest in these persons whom he will never meet. On one unfortunate occasion, while listening during a pastoral counselling session to a lady who frequently visited him to soliloquize at length, Archie had fallen asleep. "Mr. McTaggart, you are not listening to me," she squawked as she waved away his feeble denials.

Seeking to avoid interviews such as these, sick reports, requests for job references, *et al.* Archie took refuge in the house of Jane and Lewis wherein he received his usual hearty welcome from the old boy and his ever smiling wife. Their home was an oasis in spiritual and temporal terms, and after a dram of Lewis' excellent single malt, and the exchange of many pleasantries, Archie proceeded on his way, thoughts of the dreaded wedding looming on the horizon temporarily expelled from his mind.

What he did keep in mind was a promise to call in on Alice, an elderly body who was crippled. To Archie's surprise, this tiny lady was dressed to kill in a new outfit and hat, with shiny handbag at the ready as if about to go out; Archie was very puzzled because she never left the house.

"Going somewhere?" ventured Archie.

"To the wedding, of course," she explained, evidently taken aback by the question.

Wedding? That dreadful word again! *What wedding?* Archie's heart sagged like a wet sandbag. Good Lord, he had forgotten a wedding - panic station - occupational hazard.

"Whose wedding?" he asked weakly, as the contents of his stomach stirred uneasily; before pulling himself together sufficiently to address the issue thoughtfully. *Today is Wednesday, who would be getting married on a Wednesday?*

Alice continued: "Did you not know? It's Len and Rita's wedding."

Len and Rita? He didn't know any Len and Rita - or did he? Archie's absent-mindedness was often referred to by his wife, so had he forgotten them and their wedding?

"It's at seven o'clock," said Alice. It was four-thirty in the afternoon - the penny dropped for Archie to his intense relief. The wedding was on the telly. Thank God for that, he sighed as he left wee Alice all excited and dolled up for a Soap Opera wedding which was as real for her as the genuine article. Weddings, weddings, weddings, he was fed up hearing about them. Next thing, everybody in the place would be talking about this blasted Magdalene wedding, the greatest show on earth, another Soap spectacular if ever there was one. Archie was beginning to wonder if what was happening to him was real or unreal. That really worried him - was he losing the place?

Margaret was out when he returned, a note notifying him that she had gone out with her mother - he was to put his dinner in the oven, gas mark 5. Her mother - the mention of Sylvia was enough to make Archie feel that all the woes of life were relentlessly overtaking him. The silent, empty manse looked bigger than usual - the hall vast, the rooms high, cold, wide, brooding. The telephone had no recorded messages from Gordon on the answering machine to comfort and enlighten him. He gloomily heated his plate of mince and tatties, placed it on a tray, lit the gas fire, and settled down to eat. Then he switched on the television set.

Fork half way to his mouth, Archie froze stiff: there it was exploding onto the screen: Magdalene being interviewed by the B.B.C. outside a London hotel about her forthcoming wedding in a small town in the Scottish Highlands. Surrounded by the paparazzi with microphones outstretched and cameras flashing, there she was, in the flesh, playing the role of the giggling bride to be and enjoying all the publicity. Archie turned up the volume and moved in closer to the set; so that was the famous Magdalene. He beheld a slim youngish woman, of about thirty he guessed, dressed in a low cut gown which even he could tell had definitely not come out of Marks & Sparks. She was not a beauty, but had a taking smile and easy manner. Archie felt it was no disrespect for him to conclude that she was very definitely *nouveau riche*. Archie liked just about everybody he met, and Magdalene was no exception. He rather took to her. So that was the lady about to become his daughter-in-law. What would Margaret make of her?

The programme cut to a brief interview in Edinburgh with the First Minister of the Scottish Parliament. Regrettably he was unable to be present at the ceremony, but yes, he knew St. Regulus, not well, but he had heard a good deal about the town from a political acquaintance of his.

The scene then switched to a television studio in London where Lady Cynthia, the Chatelaine of Sutor House, was laying it on thick in her loud Hooray Henry voice about the great Magdalene staying at her stately home for the wedding. Finally managing to get a word in, the self-important woman doing the interviewing asked the so far unanswered question: Who was the bridegroom? Her Ladyship's feeble attempts to pretend that she was in the know on this subject merely showed that she did not know and, indeed, had never seen any reason to give the question prior thought. What 'Sin' had not considered was becoming pretty obvious to anyone who had been following events closely: St. Regulus was the place from which Gordon McTaggart came, and it was fairly well known that his father was the minister there, one of those stern, dour, Calvinist Presbyterians ministers English people read about in the rare references to Scotland which turn up in their newspapers. The bridegroom's identity was now, Archie realised, no longer the issue of the day.

"Ghastly woman," hissed Archie, switching off the TV. Look at her; she's got the backside and the lips of a horse. There she sits, Lady Bigshot, blabbing her head off and landing me right in it. Hordes of tabloid vultures will swoop down into the town, heading my way to tear out of me the names and dates and heaven knows what else concerning the bridegroom and this insufferable marriage which is about to blight my peaceful existence. The prospect was too frightful for words.

Well, the wedding was all out in the open now–so much for Veronica's big secret. He sat back getting a grip on himself, absorbing the shock of this rapidly unfolding drama. Sensing her master's struggle with distress, Pepsi, the most sensitive of canines, toddled over and laid her head on his lap and licked his hand. It was the sort of understanding support he needed.

His mind elsewhere, Archie did not hear the front door opening and closing and his dear wife calling his name. Margaret increased her volume to a shrill, commanding level: "Archie, come and help Sylvia and me bring in the message bags."

He struggled to his feet in obedience to the call; his mother-in-law had arrived, his spirits hit an all-time low, he understood the feelings of Job, and he felt that 'dark night of the soul' endured by every saint with a first-class degree in suffering sanctity.

Conversation during the ensuing ten minutes was in the interrogative mode as Sylvia assaulted Archie's ears with questions about her grandson's grandiose matrimonial intentions. The news of exciting forthcoming attractions unfolding in St. Regulus had come to Margaret and her diminutive mother via the car radio - heady stuff for an old widow woman living with a canary.

Archie did not disapprove of his mother-in-law; it was not in his nature to disapprove of people. But she did irritate him at times - she made little effort to conceal from him or anyone else that in her opinion Archie was not an award winner when it came to husbandry. As if to rub it in, she followed him about all the time: "Haunting and cleaning, haunting and cleaning, that's all your mother does here," complained Archie to his wife, "haunting and cleaning". She even had the audacity to tidy the study, his 'holy of holies'. It was more than a man can take.

Sylvia strongly disapproved not only of Archie but also of Lady Cynthia, a person she especially singled out for verbal abuse and with whom Sylvia would gladly have fought a duel to the death. Archie's reporting of seeing 'that woman' talking on television about her grandson's wedding ignited a fuse in Sylvia's bellicose nature, and it was only by Margaret's intervention that she was restrained from going round to the Big House and punching her ladyship on the nose. Small is said to be beautiful, but in

Sylvia's case - she was well over four feet tall - small was dangerous. She loved a scrap.

"Wait till I meet up with that jumped up Yah!" shouted the semi-senile dwarf, adding, "and where's that Veronica woman? She's not going to give ME the run around."

Archie buried his face in his hands; Margaret, ever the conciliator, passed a glass of sherry to her aged parent. Sylvia piped down.

The 'phone rang and Margaret sprang to get it. "Gordon?" queried Archie. "No, it's the painter for you."

The painter reported that the scaffolding had been erected round the kirk and he had a team ready to begin putting on three coats of the best white paint. It would not take long and when finished all the old stains would be gone, and it would look clean and fresh for the wedding. Archie took all this in before saying in a steely voice: "And, who I wish to know, authorised this?" The painter replied that the job had been ordered by an American lady and okayed by Mrs. McTaggart. Archie banged the 'phone down.

He eyed his wife sternly: "Did you know about this?"

Margaret started vigorously plumping up the cushions saying unperturbedly as she slapped them: "I told you all about it yesterday. You weren't listening."

The husband denied this hotly. "You most certainly did not! You had no right to…"

Margaret cut him short. "Och, don't go on - you're getting the church painted for free, and it hasn't been done for years and its going to be on television." So declaiming, she flounced out of the room, leaving Archie hissing with irritation. "It is from scenes like these old Scotia's grandeur springs…" Nature's way of ensuring and vivifying a happy marriage is for a wife not to tell, and a husband not to listen to what she did not say. As the man said when he saw a pair o' ducks: "life is a paradox."

The telephone rang again: it was the Rev. Francis Norman Stein, minister of Cloutiewell, Archie's neighbouring parish.

"Hello, Frank," said Archie breezily. The Rev. Francis did not like being called Frank: the name Frank N. Stein was something he found hard to live with. Indeed, throughout the Presbytery he was known as Frankenstein on account of his dreadful pomposity and inclination to chunter on delivering dry as toast speeches which rivalled those of Fidel Castro for lengthy statement of the blindingly obvious. In his favour, Archie used to say that he had taught his people to pray - pray that is for his departure elsewhere, anywhere! Frank was one of the few people Archie could not get along with and he could only just, with much Christian forbearance, barely abide the man at long range.

Frankenstein had a lot to say about THIS WEDDING in St. Regulus, beginning with an intimation to Archie that he was against it for the following reasons: the woman involved was a notorious sinner; the whole thing was a publicity stunt which would bring discredit to the Church of Scotland; Magdalene was already married because annulments from Rome did not apply in Scots Law. He further stated that he intended raising the matter with the Principal Clerk of the General Assembly, and concluded his summing up of the indictment by issuing an ultimatum to Archie to scratch the fixture and declare the match abandoned. To underline his points, he blew his nose vigorously into the receiver.

Archie cheered up: it was delightful to know that Frankenstein was jealous: great! He must be climbing the curtains with jealousy! The last time anyone had been so jealous of him was when Archie attended Rome for a Conference of the Old Testament Society, a learned body membership of which Archie shared with the Pope. Returning with a wee medal personally gifted to him by His Holiness, an R.C. priest of his acquaintance had been exceedingly jealous because he didn't have a wee medal from the Pope. In the spirit of ecumenism, Archie gave him the trinket, though this magnanimous gesture did not entirely eradicate the jealousy thereafter.

In the present case of the Rev. Mr. Stein's jealousy and threats, Archie was neither magnanimous nor yielding; "Stop the wedding, you say. Well I say 'Absolutely not', goodbye." With which terse, yet light-hearted words, he put down the 'phone feeling as if he had just had an eagle on a very long par five.

Overhearing, Margaret spotted a window of opportunity and cleaned it saying softly, "That put him in his place - the cheek of the man. Put off the wedding for him - not likely!"

A little deception in a good cause: Margaret's indignation masked her pleasure that the Rev. Mr. Stein's intervention had settled matters once and for all. Archie had said that he was proceeding with the wedding, and he could not back out again without being derided by that monstrous Frankenstein. Things had worked out nicely for her, but then they always did when she wanted something from her man.

"I was talking to the ladies who do the cleaning at the Crown," went on Margaret astutely changing the subject, "you know, Jessie and Sadie, and they told me a minibus full of tall young men emptied into the hotel. They must be joining the two who went about the town the other day in Highland dress. Vera said they are all

Americans, bodyguards for Magdalene when she gets here."

"More Yanks? In a minibus? What do they think they are doing? Invading Iran?" blurted out a baffled Archie who was finding the ebb and flow of his emotions hard to control. "I just wish to heavens they would all go back where they came from and take this Magdalene dame with them."

"Can't do that now, dear," soothed Margaret, "Magdalene hasn't arrived yet. Don't worry about it, darling, I'm sure Gordon will clear all this up once he telephones."

Margaret always had the last word in the McTaggart household, for although Archie was acknowledged by his 'better half' to be the head of the house; everyone knew that she was the neck which turned the head whichever way she wanted.

Archie subsided into a weak: "Well, he hasn't 'phoned yet, has he?"

"He will, he will," predicted Margaret; but that night and for the next several days, the telephone did not ring as hoped.

Meanwhile, the town buzzed like a bee hive with rumours and anticipation. What a media fest this was going to be! The oldies started asking who this Magdalene person was; the young told them, displaying an astonishingly vast amount of knowledge about her career, and millions of albums, and many Grammy Awards. Mobile 'phones swept the news across Scotland and its borders as countless teenagers planned to descend on St. Regulus with their bivouacs and caravans. With a swift efficiency not usually associated with their making arrangements, the Hielan' Authorities began to install Portaloo toilets for the tented village about to spring up on the links. Jings! Magdalene coming to "Reggie" with a following of hysterical, placard waving, pushing, shoving, cheering, swooning, videoing worshippers. All good for business: the two tearooms bought in goodies; the ladies of The Guild, under President Margaret's supervision, hired the Gladstone Hall with additional chairs and tables and cutlery and started baking for coffee mornings. It was going to be an event to rival Mecca during the hadj, or a Hindu Sunday School Trip to the Ganges. There had been nothing like it in the old town since thousands gathered on the hill to witness the battle of Culloden across the water.

In the general fervour, one question came to the fore - when exactly was this wedding? On T.V. from London, Archie watched a panel of unshaven, unkempt, glassy-eyed pop pundits in denims enthusing over Magdalene's virtues and invaluable contribution to music, taking the opportunity drop each other's names and refresh their much faded personal publicity. All spoke of Magdalene with great familiarity, assuming without question that an invitation to the wedding would be coming their way. They also spoke knowingly of the date, Gordon's participation as bridegroom, and gave the impression that, if pushed, they might be able to find Scotland on a map. This performance made those viewers interested in celebrity weddings (just about every woman in G.B.) excited and impressed. As for Archie, he was left scoffing at the effrontery of these idiots (pronounced eejits) for they had no more idea than he had when the wedding would take place, and he ought to know if anyone did. After all he was the guy conducting the wedding and it would be his signature on the Marriage Schedule when it came requiring his approval. He felt quite powerful, THE dominant figure at the centre of everything. Time people realised that.

It was now clear just how wrong all the rumour mills had been about the bridegroom; they had ground out their speculations and not one of them had seriously considered G. McTaggart for the job. As a matter of course, every one of them had predicted that Magdalene would be yoked to some handsome drummer or hunk of a song writer she had encountered in her search for true love. As for the story of her getting married in Scotland, well the bookies had given 100-1 against, and the best guess anybody had come up with in favour of her choosing that remote land was that she had seen "Braveheart" and thought it a wildly romantic sort of place for a tartan wedding. If Princess Anne chose to wed at Crathie Kirk, Balmoral, why shouldn't the Queen of Rock & Roll choose a joint like St. Regulus for her own happy day?

Archie and Margaret were not sure whether to be pleased or displeased that it had taken so long for their son to be recognized as the mysterious bridegroom. What did displease them was that it was being presented as Magdalene marrying Gordon instead of Gordon marrying Magdalene; after all, she may be a famous entertainer but, he was a prominent and distinguished member of the Government, a cabinet minister, and a future Prime Minister. But then that was all his doing: it was Gordon who had kept his name out of this and made them promise to keep it a secret. Why had he done that? They knew he was shrewd, even devious when it suited him, and had never worn his heart on his sleeve, but in this case he must have outperformed himself to keep his assignations with such a spotlight celebrity unobserved, especially as he himself was a *prominenti* in Britain and by no means unknown to the Washington Press Corps. It was, perhaps, just a passing thought, but Archie said to Margaret as they went up to bed: "I think there must be some sort of conspiracy going on here. What's Gordon up to?"

"Whatever it is, there's some funny business going on," said mother in confirmation.

Came the dawn, and with it the world's press. Top of the range hacks looked up St. Regulus on their satellite navigation systems and beamed in by the dozen. If the wedding was in this remote village in the tundra of northern Scotland, then the local vicar, the Rev. McTaggart, would know the whereases and the wherefores. *Ask not for whom the 'phone tolls, It tolls for thee;* the manse telephone rang its first maddening tocsin at first light of day. As the McTaggart's were sidelining this aural bombardment into their answering machine, editors in many lands were scrambling their ace reporters for the flight to Inverness.

Andy, the "Reggie" newsagent shop proprietor, opened early and immediately sold out his stock of tabloids, every one of which printed Magdalene on their front cover dressed in a miniskirt long enough to create interest and short enough to cover the essentials. "Highland Fling" squealed the headline. The Scottish 'quality' newspapers discretely placed the same picture of Magdalene's saucy, semi-clad performances on page 2; their Culture sections interviews with the star revealed that, having seen that great Scottish play "Peter Pan", and sung at New Year's Bobby Burns song "Auld Lang Zine", she loved Scotland. In the editorial columns of the English newspapers, incomprehension was expressed that the world's most glamorous entertainer was not to be married in a high-class London Registry Office (as befits anybody who is anybody) but in 'The Provinces' and by a Presbyterian minister at that. The standard caricature of himself and his fellow ministers as a frightfully dour lot made Archie shake his head - what an eccentric lot the chattering classes are, shallow people terrified of being thought 'religious'. And then you had the High Anglicans, all smells and bells, terrified J. Calvin is hiding under the bed. Of course, he did not include any Royal Marines in this analysis - the English among them were above all such criticisms.

What irked Archie most of all were media references to Gordon being a dismal Johnny Scots' skinflint unfit to become Prime Minister of the United Kingdom. Gordon was scathingly called 'a son of the manse', and although Southern journalists had no idea what a manse is, it sounded Calvinistic and that was enough to send shudders of revulsion through the ranks of the London Establishment.

Hacks began appearing at the manse door and peering through the windows. They soon discovered that the minister possessed a very fine sense of humour, was anything but dour, had been decorated with the Military Cross, and that Archie, having studied the works and life of John Calvin, held that great scholar in high regard - with, of course, reservations over the more outdated aspects of his theology (after all, Calvin was French, a foreigner, and not British). They also learnt that Archie held the boxing medal from 45 Commando, Royal Marines, Arbroath, and that aggressive questioning on their part would be not be advisable.

CHAPTER EIGHT

Closing In

The most pressing thing Archie and Margaret wanted to know at the moment was where had Veronica gone? After an absence of three days they learnt that she was returned from wherever she had been with the Marquis, and had headed straight for Sutor House. Having just returned herself from London, her Ladyship was available to meet Veronica and receive from her a legal contract for accommodation for Magdalene and her entourage, the rental to be paid in advance. As Veronica wrote out a cheque for an enormous sum (small change to her employer), Cynthia signed on the dotted, and was immediately told that Magdalene's bedroom furnishings would be delivered and installed in the appropriate quarters that very afternoon. A glance at the cheque persuaded its recipient that this un-contracted measure was not sufficiently inconvenient to raise objections. The moving in of staff and others, Veronica said, would take place shortly.

"And the day of the wedding will be…?" asked the lady of the House, not a little flustered by the speed of events. Veronica assured her that once the arrangements had been agreed with the minister she would be one of the first to know – an unsatisfactory reply, but the best Cynthia was going to get for now. Business done, Veronica screwed the top on her gold pen and snapped her brief case shut.

Archie was not at home when Veronica turned up at the manse, pushing her way through the throng of reporters pressing microphones into her face. Having watched, through his binoculars, the Marquis entering the harbour in his speedboat he had gone round to his place to find out where the Frenchman and Veronica had been and what they were up to - suspicions were growing on Archie hourly.

Taking the wee old lady who opened the door to be the cleaning woman, Veronica pushed past her into the safety of the vestibule and enquired, somewhat breathlessly, if Mr. McTaggart was in residence.

"No, he's no in," barked the wee woman like a yapping West Highland terrier with a grievance. "You'll be thon American woman, come away in."

Veronica concluded from this introduction that this initial encounter required tact and caution on her own part, for this person must be none other than the targe of a mother of whom Margaret had spoken.

"Is Maggi, I mean Mrs. McTaggart available?" she asked meekly. To this she received no reply, and was shooed into Archie's study.

"Look at this place - a disgrace," said the midget, "I told her not to marry him."

From there she was led into what Veronica took to be the old dame's bedroom to be shown a cage in which was perched a very unhappy canary. This poor bird was completely naked except for one feather. Veronica, never having seen a canary denuded of feathers was moved to pity, for the poor thing was reduced from a size 10 with its clothes on to a size 1 disrobed. Without its feathers, there is not much canary left to see, and what there is looks exceedingly skinny.

"It never whistles now," sighed old mother whatever her name was, looking as unhappy as the silent siffleur.

Veronica felt called upon to express a few words of consolation to the unhappy songster which had lost feathers and whistle. V's training in the art of communication had not included speaking to sick canaries in the presence of a wild-eyed geriatric canary lover, but she guessed that a few additional tut-tuts would help place herself in a favourable light. This was hoping for too much.

"He's neglected that poor birdie ever since you came here," snarled the midget. "It's worried sick, thanks to you."

By now Veronica was beginning to adjust to the fact that she had met a demented enemy of Archie, and that she herself was being held personally responsible for the nervous breakdown of a canary which had resulted in a moulting of feathers, chirp loss, and shivering hypothermia.

"What a shame," she said for want of anything better to say, then expanded the sentiment with the after-thought: "stress can have a psychosomatic effect upon people too, you know - not that people have feathers, but if they did, they would lose them like this sad little creature God has made." Veronica rarely spoke foolish words, and these were not only downright silly but most annoying, for she knew as she uttered them that she was leaving herself wide open to her titchy companion's verbal darts.

"What you havering about woman? Feathers? People? Are you stupid girl? Tell Archie to get the vet."

The welfare of canaries had never been numbered amongst Veronica's charitable concerns, but she had a vague memory of having seen a film called "The Birdman of Alcatraz" and was not without tender feelings towards fluffy chicks and ducklings and other feathered friends.

"I will see to it that the little fellow gets the best treatment available, no matter the cost. We can't have this," she added for emphasis, though how exactly one can treat a canary for psychiatric problems was a question she did not raise. *Why on earth could anybody think her arrival was worrying canaries to death? This was a crazy place, full of screwballs.*

Having seen Daft Willie with a whirligig on what passed for a brain, and having concluded that the Colonel and his weird butler were of unsound mind, now she was meeting Margaret's cuckoo mother and an anxiety prone canary!

"My name is Veronica," she said as amiably as possible.

"I know who you are," shot back the reply.

"And you are?" tartly retaliated Veronica.

"Sylvia", the feisty one conceded.

Holding all the conversational cards, Sylvia changed the subject: "Which University did you attend, a reputable one by American standards, I hope?"

Trying not to further bristle at this impertinence Veronica frostily replied: "Harvard Law School. After graduation I was at Yale, where I majored in Business Studies; and then I moved on to Princeton where I took a Ph.D. in English Literature."

"Quite satisfactory," Sylvia said like an approving headmistress. "And tell me; is Sir Walter Scott still the doyen of English literature?"

"Of course," affirmed Veronica figuring this was the right thing to say, "His popularity and readership are always growing." Covering her retreat with smiles of peace and looks of love, she edged towards the door hoping to escape from the dotty old dame.

"You will be re-roofing the church," said Sylvia.

This lady is a lot smarter than I realized. Caught off guard and cornered, Veronica, could only answer: "Of course, but not, I'm afraid in time for the wedding."

"Facts are chiels that winna ding," responded Sylvia, mystifying her hearer. Then, she put the knife in:

"You are up to something here Miss, I can tell. You can't fool me."

Veronica knew the woman was right: she was indeed 'up to something', though she would have preferred not to put it that way herself. She certainly presented herself as the model professional business woman which, indeed, she was, but the perceptive Sylvia saw through all that - the Veronica woman was up to something.

Margaret's return home at that point was both welcome and timely for Veronica. The somewhat fraught conversation with Sylvia dried up, and the old bird went off in to do some haunting and cleaning elsewhere in the house.

"See you met my mother," said Margaret, breathless after running the gauntlet of journalists outside.

V ventured: "Is she a bit…?"

Margaret laughed: "My mother? Senile Dementia? Believe me; she's as sharp as a razor. She doesn't miss a trick."

"I kinda gathered that," said V soberly.

While V and Maggi were engaged in excited conversation about the forthcoming wedding, Archie was passing the Crown Hotel on his way to the Marquis house on the Shore Road. Seeing an unoccupied police car outside the hostelry, he concluded correctly that the two local gendarmes were inside, and entered to join them.

He found them taking down notes from as tough a gang of mobsters as he had ever seen in the gangster movies of his youth. The place seemed full of James Cagneys and Al Capones. Shirt-sleeved, some were playing poker and smoking cigars – he considered it prudent not to bring the 'No Smoking' sign to their attention. These recently arrived employees of Magdalene had certainly made themselves at home, offering the Bobbies whisky from the bar to which they had gained free access. The atmosphere was pleasant, jovial, and Police Constables Eddie and Big Jimmy seemed satisfied with whatever information they had been given, and instructions they had been delivering. They paid no attention to the shoulder holsters slung over chairs which Archie noted. He also observed that the two peripatetic kilties who had earlier toured the town now wore trousers having discovered that Highland dress is not everyday wear in Scotland. They had also discovered to their surprise that practically all Scots spoke English for their first, and indeed, only language.

Archie was offered, and accepted, a hospitable dram from this cast of characters out of Hell's Kitchen and The Godfather. With underlying Sicilian deference for the priesthood, Archie was given that most precious of all Mafia gestures, namely respect, and introduced "real nice" to the gorilla he took to be the don, a character who reminded him of Harry the Horse in Damon Runyan's stories of old Broadway. After the "How ya doin', man" phase of this encounter, Archie excused himself with promises to meet up with 'the guys' as soon as possible, and retreated with the boys in blue out of the smoke and into the street.

They had little light to shed on the fortified encampment which had formerly been the Crown Hotel, an establishment noted for its genteel summer clientele, and high teas for better-off tourists. The orders they had received from on high (i.e. Highland Constabulary) were simply to co-operate with the incomers. As for the Americans, they had vouchsafed little information beyond saying they were Magdalene's bodyguards and accompanied her on her travels; it seems there had been several attempts on her life unreported in the press. Who these mercenary hoodlums were the two gendarmes did not say for they had not asked, having no curiosity about matters which did not offer opportunities for overtime. Accordingly, the pair drove off to fight crime in some other part of the world.

It was becoming increasingly clear to Archie that some clandestine operation was taking place right under his nose. This dame my son is about to wed needs bodyguards! Well, when he thought about it, it made sense: they say that big-time performers don't get to the top in Las Vegas without sponsorship by the Mob, and he had seen a programme about Frank Sinatra on the T.V. to prove it. The possibility of Magdalene being 'rubbed out' in his parish by persons unknown made him realize she was somebody's valuable asset, a commodity investment providing a regular income worth preserving. Archie was beginning to feel distinctly uncomfortable and worried: what on earth was Gordon getting himself into?

By the time he arrived at the nearby house of the Marquis farther along the road, Archie's anxiety had acquired a new urgency and he began his questioning as soon as the door was opened: Where did the Marquis get a speedboat to go off with Veronica? Where did they go? Where did they stay for two days? What were they doing going off like that?

It did not completely surprise Archie (he was getting well used to surprises) to be told that the Marquis and Veronica had known each other before she came to St. Regulus and knew each other very well at that. They had met in Hollywood, and at the Cannes Film Festival, and many other celebrity events in the film business. Or so the Marquis said; Archie was taking all he was told these days with a shovel full of salt.

The speedboat? Oh, the Sheikh had provided that and he had arranged accommodation. Veronica had wanted to take a look at Auchenshuggle Castle, and he went along for the ride. These answers in the musical French accent of the Marquis sounded as beguilingly plausible as Maurice Chevalier singing "Gigi", but Archie had other questions on his mind which was bothering him, like - why are you lying to me? And what the hell's going on here?

The Marquis just happens to be in St. Regulus, of all places, when his old pal Veronica turns up by coincidence - does he really think I'm daft enough to believe that? By now, Archie was fully convinced some sort of intrigue was afoot, and he was going to find out what it was. As a young minister in his first charge, Archie had once been threatened by a schism in the congregation, and, with military alacrity, he had suppressed the rebellion forcefully, acting decisively as a good Commando does on all occasions. So now he resolved to seek out and confront Veronica and interrogate her as to her activities on behalf of the unseen Magdalene in relationship to his missing elder son.

A ring of the Marquis' doorbell took him thither and Archie overheard him involved in a whispered conversation of a conspiratorial nature with the unseen new arrival. When Veronica entered the room, it was apparent that she had already been made aware that Archie was present and asking questions. A beautiful woman can always disarm a man, and when Veronica turned on the charm, her blandishments were irresistible, but Archie was not taken in by the feigned surprise she showed at seeing him with the Marquis.

"Everything all right over at Auchenshuggle Castle?" enquired Archie, with a touch of sarcasm which did not escape her.

She gave a quick glance towards the Marquis, unsure what he had already said to Archie on the subject.

"Oh, yes," she smiled, "the Sheikh was not present but his family and the ladies of the harem treated us royally didn't they Henri?" *Oh yes,* thought Archie - *now it's Henri, is it?*

"You didn't stay at the castle, you stayed at the Drum Hotel," said Archie who knew this because the landlord, his golfing friend Jim White, had 'phoned to tell him so, being curious about his two guests from St. Regulus.

"Alterations are being made to the castle," explained the quick witted Marquis. Veronica shifted uncomfortably.

Archie let it go at that. He was tempted to ask where the Sheikh's family and harem had lodged, but he knew it was irrelevant, so he moved on.

"When's the wedding?" he persisted icily, getting to the point.

"Ah, the wedding arrangements," replied Veronica, promptly recovering the composure of a Portia, "I called at your manse to discuss this but you were here, of course. Magdalene will be arriving next Friday for the wedding on Saturday. Naturally, the Service will be at a time suitable to you. 14.00 hours is suggested. I do hope this is acceptable. If you are otherwise engaged, and unable to conduct the ceremony, Magdalene's sister could conduct the wedding."

If there was one thing calculated to bring Archie to the boil it was to be told when and where a wedding in his kirk has been arranged without his knowledge. Fussy brides and bossy bridegrooms were anathema to the Rev. Mr. McTaggart, especially when they tried telling him what and what not to do at a wedding. As for Magdalene's sister taking the wedding, that was a declaration of war! Veronica, no doubt accustomed to pliable pastors in her homeland across the pond, had assumed that Scots Presbyterian ministers of religion can be ordered up like any other article of merchandise and paid C.O.D. She was therefore taken aback by Archie ferocious reaction. She swiftly took note that for once she had misread a situation, and scolded herself for forgetting the P.R. lectures she had received in dealing with the customs of foreign nationals.

"Of course," she meekly placated, "Magdalene would never dream of acting without your complete approval, and we will follow your instructions and advice fully."

That's better, thought Archie, never a difficult man to placate, so he cooled down and recovered his authority; with the words: "I'll let you know" by which he meant that Mrs McT. would tell him what to do. As he always did when people pressed dates upon him, Archie played for time...*let's see, this is Wednesday and she wants Saturday....there is a club competition that day so I and the Colonel won't miss a game...*he kept a stern face for Veronica but thought that Saturday first didn't look too bad.

"I'll let you know," he said again, this time in a lighter voice which Veronica took as a 'Yes', and a dismissal. So she glided off in her most Vassar trained, lady-like manner, distributing maidenly farewells as she passed through the door. A jiffy later, she popped her head back in again like Lieutenant Colombo to say: "By the way, The President is sending Secretary of State Marjorie Alright to represent him at the wedding. You understand, her arrival is Top Secret for security reasons, so please, we are only told this on 'a need to know basis' and must not breathe a word in public." So saying she hurried back round to the manse to see Maggi and persuade her to keep up the good work of winning her husband over.

Suddenly Archie felt himself to be an even more important man than he had thought - *Secretary of State of the U.S.A., eh.* How his stock would rise in Presbytery and at the golf club. *Frankenstein's gas would be turned down to a peep!*

Veronica gone, he continued questioning the Marquis with strong insistence and along the lines of: "So you know Veronica well do you? What about our Magdalene?" - Archie felt he was beginning to talk about this woman as if he knew her.

"Met her too, Henri?" he said in a mocking voice.

The Marquis was not taking the bait: "Mais qui, of course, you know I am a script and song writer so we have met several times professionally. We are friends: I was at her second wedding in Reno, they have 'The Bijou Chapel' there for weddings."

Picturing the Las Vegas he had seen in "Ocean's Eleven", the glitzy film in which Dean Martin, Sammy Davis Junior, and other members of 'the rat pack' rob a casino, Archie assumed that Reno was the same sort of hell-hole and shuddered to imagine the crass vulgarity of a wedding in 'The Little Chapel'.

The Marquis and Archie understood each other well, not only from close acquaintance, and many a chess match, but because each could tell that the other had been highly trained in interrogation techniques. Archie pressed on searching for his opponent's weak point.

"If you don't mind me asking, what brought you to St. Regulus? Was it you who got Magdalene to come here for her third wedding?"

Gallic *hauteur* made Henri stiffen, his face clouded over at this slight upon his motives and intention: "Non, Monsieur McTaggart, I did not ask Madame Magdalene to come here. As for this being her third wedding, I must advise you that this is not her third wedding but her second. Her first 'usband died, and her second marriage was annulled so she is a widow woman. For myself, I am here for the peace and the quietness only, and meeting V and my friend Magdalene here is, how you say, pure co-incidence."

Aye, that will be right, thought Archie.

"I see, so, you knew Veronica through show business, and this Magdalene woman the same way. I've got that much."

He probed deeper: "Who is she marrying, will you tell me that - on a 'need to know basis', because I need to know?" The temperature of the exchanges was beginning to rise like a cat's back; the Marquis knew that Archie already knew who the bridegroom was, and Archie knew that the Marquis knew that he knew, so Mon Dieu! stop these stupid pretences. He glared at Archie and began pacing the room. What Archie now knew beyond any doubt was that the Marquis was involved in some sort of plot, though exactly what he was not saying. Now that he thought of it, he did not even know this Henri's surname - that is if, being a Marquis, he had a surname.

"The bridegroom's name? I believe that is a state secret," said Henri, standing there as if somebody was burning brown paper under his nose. "Veronica has no reason to tell me, and I have no wish to know. Do you know mon ami?"

This counter-attack left Archie with no alternative but to offer this touchy aristocrat, who seemed to be contemplating challenging Archie to a duel with pistols, an evasive reply: "I think so, but it has to be confirmed - might be just a rumour."

Time to go before things got out of hand. Questions for the Marquis remained, but would keep for later; Archie had enough to figure out for the moment. He glanced at the Louis XIVth clock on the mantelpiece, *paid plenty for that*, thought Archie, saying: "Just look at the time! Must go." The Marquis did not show him to the door.

It had been just about the strangest morning in Archie's life: the mobsters at The Crown, Veronica knowing the Marquis and vice-versa, the stampede towards this super-star wedding with top brass Yanks, and Sheiks in the offing.

The media wolves were howling at the manse door as he arrived back home with his head spinning - getting out an upturned helicopter underwater during his Royal Marine Commando training course had been a piece of cake compared with this wedding, at least there was a way out of the helicopter if you knew what you were doing, but now he didn't know what he was doing and there was no way out of this mess.

As he hurried home, the Q.E.2 sailed majestically through the narrow channel between the two high hills which formed a gateway into the Firth, hills from which Sutor House took its ancient name. Sailing up close to the shore, crowds on both sides of the Firth cheered and the passengers on board lined the rails to wave back; the great Queen of the oceans, towering high in the water, making a very impressive, unforgettable sight. She would soon disembark her hordes of wealthy, excited passengers on the long Inverport pier at the far end of the Firth, and they would head post-haste for Archie's wee town now made world famous, thanks to a woman he had never met, knew next to nothing about, and about whom he cared even less. Good for the bank and the shops, I suppose, he thought, for even in his darkest hours, it was in Archie's nature to consider the welfare of his flock.

A cheque awaited him on his return home for enough money to re-roof all the kirks in Scotland. This was most pleasing, a ray of sunshine on this hitherto bleak day. Archie felt himself warming towards this Magdalene; she seemed a decent lassie, and might well turn out to be a golfer. With the cheque there was a note from his wife ('Mrs Neverin' Archie called her for she was never in) which informed him that Margaret had gone to Inverness shopping. *Hope Veronica's paying,* he thought, for as he had often said on Monday evenings at The Men's Circle enjoying a hand of solo whist: 'City shopping is a wife's paradise, and a husband's hell.' This declaration was always passed unanimously by the all male company with no abstentions.

"She will be looking for a hat and an expensive outfit for this wedding," he said, talking to the note as he picked up a black bag sitting on the hall table.

It was a sealed diplomatic bag and he turned it over. The seal was broken so he took out a letter from Gordon and eagerly read the message for which he had been impatiently waiting. As he expected, Margaret had already beat him to it to read: *"Wedding Saturday. Cannot disclose more due to security reasons. Will stay Friday night at home. Looking forwards to see you both. Gather Arthur told you he is to be best man. Love, Gordon."*

Well, it wasn't much to go on but it was something; Gordon really was going to get married and it was not a hoax. Carrying the message into his study, he poured himself a small whisky, sat back in his armchair and then, the wife being out, got up again to lock the door for privacy as Prof. Jimmy Stewart, "Jonah", had advised (shot down during the Battle of Britain and by chance fished out of the English Channel by a passing trawler Jimmy had acquired from his students the nickname "Jonah"). Archie kept a photograph of him in R.A.F. uniform alongside portraits of his other heroes: Denis Law, Groucho Marx, Ken Dodd, Robert Burns, and Jim Baxter.

He rested awhile and then toddled round to the kirk. The graveyard was filled with photographers noisily fitting up huge telescopic cameras on the mossy, ancient gravestones under which the rude forefathers of the village were trying in vain to get some sleep. They flocked round him, asking for a few words, so Archie directed their attention towards a small gravestone outside the entrance to the cemetery. Explaining it was the last resting place of a man named Wilson who, anxious to get to the judgment seat on judgment day ahead of the pack so he could right a grievance, had had himself buried outside so he could get off to a flying start. By this oft-told story, Archie suggested indirectly but effectively that the paparazzi should get out of his Kirk yard immediately or he would have them arrested and judged a public nuisance. They were thick-skinned fellows by nature and profession, but they cleared off to the newly opened Sutor Arms public house which was replacing The Crown.

The vestry in the venerable old church provided Archie with asylum from the madding crowd outside and the tussling thoughts inside his mind. The tiny vestry had not much to offer in the way of comfort, the furniture being heavy early crude Victorian solid - one chair, one desk, one cast off wooden font no longer for the use of. An apostolic succession of yellowed photographs lined the wall, a long row of his bewhiskered predecessors looking down on Archie to see if he was fit to join them when the Lord called. In the absolute silence found only in the vestry of a country church, Archie sat looking up at this parade of the predeceased, men of *gravitas and pietas*, ministers of serious purpose who, in their day and generation had preached hell-fire, and dangled sinners over the pit, giving them a whiff of the sulphur for the health of their souls. Under their stern but noble gaze, Archie reflected on the course of events and his plans to deal firmly with them.

CHAPTER NINE

Sanctuary

Archie's wee kirk stood on the site of the Celtic monastery founded, according to ancient tradition, by St. Regulus in the Fifth century, his bones being reputedly buried below the pulpit. What had begun as a small collection of beehive cells had been an outpost of the Cluniacs until the community fizzled out in 1560 (they hadn't a Clue-niac, punned Archie). The present Church of Scotland was built as one of the very first post-Reformation kirks, and one of the famous 'T-shaped' places of Reformed worship. It was what Archie often told visitors: "A good place to pray."

As he reflected upon the history of this age-old sacred edifice he felt matters falling into perspective.

Here, from the pulpit, the doughty Rev. Dr. Ebenezer MacVicar had scolded the greatest of all Englishmen, Oliver Crowell, for winning the Battle of Dunbar and occupying MacVicar lands. The sermon lasted two hours, until an officer beside the Lord Protector drew his pistol proposing to shoot "the cur". Oliver stayed his hand, invited Ebenezer to lunch and personally offered a grace lasting two hours. This did not impress the good Rev, for his next grace lasted two and a quarter hours, so he emerged a clear winner and the Battle of Dunbar defeat was avenged a wee bit if not a lot.

It was from the pulpit of St. Regulus Parish Church that the Right Rev. Robert C. Nesbitt had denounced the Jacobite rebellion of 1745 and called the Bonny Prince a Papist Bastard. A Glaswegian, this champion of Whiggery was enraged by the Young Pretender's robbing of his native city, twice at that, leaving the citizens without a sock between them and a shirt to

116

their backs. When a minister of his acquaintance joined the rebels, Rab squared up to the traitor saying: "I wull tell you this," and shot him dead with an army issue Brown Bess. Tried and convicted for murder, he was transported to Australia where he fathered thirty-six children and founded the city of Melbourne. His statue now stands in Sydney having been delivered to the wrong city by mistake.

On the wall the bewhiskered portrait of the Rev. Hamish MacBurger looked down upon Archie. This stern man moved to rural Pennsylvania in the 18th century to establish a puritanical sect which renounced all things modern; rejecting the motorcar, and even the bicycle, grim adherents of this society, soberly dressed in black suits, can still be seen today driving into town by horse and buggy. They call themselves the 'Hamish People'.

As he ran his eye over the long line of illustrious ministers of St. Regulus who had gone before him, Archie was able to take a long-term view of his present situation. Soon this wedding would be over and gone leaving behind only a fleeting memory: *"The moving finger writes and having writ moves on."* As Omar Khayyam put it, and put it so well. Then he could get back to his golf.

Comforted to think that all was not lost, Archie gave thought to what he would say in his homily to the couple during the Wedding Service. The text: "Art thou he that should come, or look we for another" had been floating into his head during the time of Gordon's annoying absence and, as he couldn't better it, he settled for that. He scribbled some notes, but it was a warm afternoon, the venerable small kirk's wooden galleries creaked a lullaby and after three verses Archie nodded off.

As he slept, the whole world was reading newspapers and magazine supplements featuring Magdalene *seminudus* on page 3. Hearing from passersby that Archie was most likely to be found seeking sanctuary in his vestry, Veronica and Magdalene's sister made their way there. He was brought to consciousness by the clanking of the big iron latch on the door and the sight of Veronica accompanied by an extraordinary looking female in a dog-collar. Well aware that in Presbyterian Scotland a woman minister dressed in a black trouser suit would be suspected of being a transvestite, Veronica had dressed her companion in a smart blue skirt and blouse. The effect upon Archie would have been pleasing had Magdalene's sis borne even the slightest physical resemblance to her slim-line junior sibling, but she did not. Veronica introduced him to a fat woman named 'Darlene' who was of over-ripe years, not a lot over four feet tall, squat from heaving around a steamroller sized bosom, and wearing what Archie took to be a bottle-opener around her neck but which turned out to be brass cross. She glad-handed him, saying in a slow drawl exuding Southern hospitality: "How y'all, Rev. McTaggart? We're gonna have some real quality time together, yah hear?" Archie took her hand as if taking an electric shock. This was the female with whom he was to share his son's wedding ceremony?

Veronica stepped in saying with practiced skill: "Darlene would love to share this wonderful occasion with you, Mr. McTaggart - would it be in order for her to read a poem by Magdalene's favourite poetess, Ella Wheeler Wilcox? It is a love poem called, "Love Is In Their Eyes". It is based on St. Paul's Chapter 13 of 1st Corinthians." Archie remained motionless, as she continued: "Darlene has also chosen a hymn, 'Bind Us Together'. You will be familiar with the poem and of the hymn, of course." After winning the struggle to refrain from howling out loud with anguish of the soul, Archie quietly muttered that, although neither lyric was known to him, he would assent to the request. Nothing is ever so bad that it could not be worse, his mother had once told him, so he was relieved that Marlene (or was it Darlene?) was not intending to sing whilst accompanying herself on the geetar.

Sensing their departure would be welcome, Veronica hustled the matronly Darlene off to Sutor House, leaving Archie to remember with some amusement the aphorism: "She was only a Southern Belle, but nobody tolled her".

As the two women hobbled uphill, hot and puffed, to the doors of the Georgian pile,   Lady Cynthia emerged wearing a long white dress and a sash of Clan McSutor tartan. All smiles and cordiality, Her Ladyship graciously approached them with outstretched hand delicately poised for reception. Very much impressed Darlene made an attempt to curtsey but once down could not get back up until V. helped her, compounding the embarrassment by kissing Cynthia on the cheek, and complimenting Her Ladyship's dress saying: "Gee! Ain't that cool?" The result was that Cynthia's warm welcome suddenly fell below freezing. The idea of this common female cleric with a vulgar name staying beneath her ornamented roof was a sacrifice of good taste which only money could justify. In short, Darlene was as unpopular with Cynthia as a bald man in a barber's shop. However, unpopularity with Cynthia practically guaranteed a big hit with His Lordship, who, upon discovering that Darlene was a keen gardener, took her to his heart and to see his roses.

Veronica then undertook the delicate task of explaining to her hostess that Magdalene's staff and relatives were about to arrive; these would not be, as Cynthia had presumed, French chefs, uniformed maids, and liveried footmen. They would take the form of Magdalene's relatives from back home in West Virginia, country folks with a fondness for barbecued fried chicken and cheese burgers. Lady Cynthia shuddered and reeled slightly; Veronica held out a firm and steadying hand, the tight grip letting it be known that, as a well-bred New Englander, she fully shared Cynthia's repugnance for banjo playing, tobacco chewing, moonshine distilling, Hill Billys. Cynthia, needing a friend at this hour of calamity, developed a sudden fondness for Veronica, and they passed indoors for afternoon tea in the splendour of the Great Hall.

Returning to the manse by a back route which avoided the streets now packed with rubber-necking trippers, Archie was given a cheerful welcome by Margaret who was giving her new hat for the wedding a trial run. This large creation of some exuberant milliner pleased her no end until doubts about her choice crept in: she stopped looking in the mirror for a moment to turn to Archie and ask in an anxious voice if he considered she had made a good selection. Assurances by her husband, skilled in answering such dubieties, that her choice was admirable and beyond improvement, Margaret went on to notify him that every hotel for miles around was booked up, and the roads jammed with traffic. The excitement was building every hour. She was very nearly as nervously thrilled as on her own wedding day, and that was saying something. She gave the hat another once over.

Archie slipped away for a few holes before bedtime, while Margaret, after enthusiastically explaining for several hours on the telephone to her countless lady friends that her son was about to marry the famous Magdalene, retired to her bath and the formulation of plans and designs for the decoration of the kirk with flowers. Archie returned pleased at his improved putting stroke, and so to bed, his arms around his soul-mate of many years.

He was nodding off peacefully when, as was her custom, she started up her pillow talk: "Archie," she whispered, "does all this seem real and above board to you?"

He grunted peevishly, as was his custom on these occasions.

She carried on regardless: "There's something going on here we haven't been told about, isn't there? Does it sound fishy to you, dear?"

"Fishy," he echoed from far away.

"When you were in the Royal Marines you must have been familiar with the operations of Special Forces and all those cloak and dagger things they do."

He made no reply, turned over, and left Margaret to lie wide awake, thinking of Alex Guinness in "Smiley's People" while quietly saying to her sleeping spouse "Fishy...Yes...very fishy."

CHAPTER TEN

Action Stations

In the brilliant sunshine of the Friday early morning, the USS Capitol Hill anchored her hundred-thousand tons of aircraft-carrier in the deep water off St. Regulus. She was the largest warship ever seen in the Firth, far bigger than any of the mighty battleships which had anchored there in days gone by. This colossus, which could have contained the whole of Washington's Capitol Hill, dome and all, was carrying more aircraft that the entire French air force - a fact divulged proudly to Archie and Margaret by the Admiral when they boarded her for lunch at his invitation. Veronica was also present (what's she doing here? thought Archie), as was the local M.P. (pompous ass must be here because of Gordon, thought Archie). They were piped aboard this awesome vessel with due ceremony and much friendliness. Archie, no stranger to American warships, for he had had gone on many N.A.T.O. training exercises with the U.S. Marine Corps, wore his medals and looked around to see if he recognized anyone. The ship's chaplain, a U.S. Marine, greeted Archie like a long-lost cousin, for here was one of his own in that closed brotherhood of Commandos and Special Forces.

Lunch went extremely well: the food from the high-class galley, washed down by non-alcoholic wines, went down singing hymns and the Admiral was most cheerful and pleasant. Wives are ever ready to act as the spokesperson for their husbands and so it was that Margaret, in the well-intentioned hope of bonding more closely our boys and theirs, proudly announced that Archie was a former Marine. This information was received by the company at table in a chilling silence, for sailors and marines, in any navy, are not chummy. The Admiral scowled; he had not forgotten being denied a cabin by the Royal Marines and was obliged to sleep on a mattress on the deck of a Limey ship during his visit to Plymouth. Such snubs rankle with sailors, especially Admirals, and they cry out for revenge. But happily, on this one occasion, the old Sea Dog decided to pardon Margaret's gaffe for it was obvious from her bewildered looks that she knew not what she had done wrong; and diplomacy was required. He was an Admiral on a goodwill cruise, showing the flag, attending the wedding at the behest of the White House, so he bit the bullet and smiled. American hospitality in all its lavish generosity continued and was appreciated in full by his guests who expressed awe at the size of his vessel. A brief tour prompted Archie to comment that all it lacked was a motorway, a remark which went some short way towards helping the Admiral to think slightly better of marines.

Over coffee in the ward room (no drinkies, the U.S. Navy is 'dry' explained Archie), Veronica raised the question of seating at the wedding: in the somewhat restricted space of the kirk, she said, she had allocated second row seats for the Admiral and Senior officers. They would sit directly behind the Secretary of State. As she spoke in her usual, brisk, businesslike fashion, a signal was handed to the ship's captain notifying him that the occupant of that high office had just arrived, having landed on the flight deck in a Chinook and disembarked surrounded by her attendant posse of officials.

This news left Archie and wife overwhelmed; Veronica had told them that Marjorie Alright was coming, but that such a renowned figure had actually arrived in St. Regulus seemed impossible to believe. That the President of the most powerful nation on earth would send a nuclear aircraft-carrier and a top official to a wedding in their wee kirk was an honour indeed. Margaret had the thrilling feeling that she was appearing by magic in her favourite T.V. programme 'The West Wing'; here was the drama, with all its intrigues, not on the 'telly', but in real life and she was playing a part in it. The Oval Office brought right here into her own home; it was all too fantastic to be true, yet it really was happening to her. She pinched herself.

The great lady was introduced; when Margaret was eagerly asked later what the Secretary of State was like to meet as a person, Margaret would say of this walking, talking, breathing embodiment of a super-power: "She is very nice, not a bit pretentious. She goes to Wimbledon every year. We talked a lot about tennis and family. I liked her." The nearest Margaret's friends and acquaintances had ever come to such a prestigious individual was on the Six o'clock T.V. news, so in the school staff-room and at the Guild, her stock pinnacled and she basked in the reflected glory.

Ms. Alright was not a bit like her nickname; 'Saddam's Granny'. Instead of looking and behaving like Rocky Marciano in a bad mood, she was, as Margaret readily testified, extremely pleasant, open, and easy to talk to (or talk with, as our transatlantic cousins put it). She was no chicken; of medium height, well proportioned and slightly thickened at the hips, her plain face was rendered attractive by sparkling eyes, and perfectly groomed hair. Carrying herself with an unmistakable air of authority, she had 'class', something her compatriots admire because so few of them in public life possess it.

Though carried away by this superior dame from the New World, Margaret registered, with a discerning feminine eye, that the Secretary of State, though an accomplished woman and credit to her sex, nevertheless lacked the charisma so graciously exemplified by our own dear Queen. Margaret had been introduced to Her Majesty at the Garden Party of the General Assembly of the Church of Scotland in Edinburgh, and as she told one and all emphatically ever since that memorable day: "The Queen may be tiny, but she is every inch a queen." Wealth and politics can gain a talented person position and power, but never will they rise to regal status; Marjorie Alright was all right, and more than all right - a great person, in fact, but not well bred, not royal.

For his part, Archie was not much of a royalist. The Queen? Yes, definitely charismatic. The rest of them? Aristocratic spongers. American politicians? Well, some might be okay but most of them were scoundrels. Ms. Alright seemed okay. He made a mental note to ask Gordon about her and what she was doing here. Seemed a big deal to send someone so important to a wedding - was it Magdalene who was the draw? Or was it Gordon with his prospects of leading America's closest ally? Whatever it was, sending an air-craft carrier for their wedding was well over the top; even sending a cruiser seemed a bit much to Archie who had been to sea and done the rounds. The story that this huge ship happened to be around on N.A.T.O. exercises and just happened to be available to call in at St. Regulus definitely did not wash - no way. It merely clinched Archie's suspicions that there was much more going on here than met the eye.

"I hope," said Margaret to V, waving the White Ensign, "I hope that representatives of the Royal Navy will be in attendance at the wedding."

Veronica looked at the Admiral, the Admiral looked at one of his aides, and the aide concerned looked at Margaret as he nodded smartly and uttered assurances that Margaret's navy would, indeed, be represented and that for good measure the Loyal Toast to the Queen would be given at the reception. Margaret found herself in full agreement with this proposal, so she indicated that that was fine with her.

The Laird and his wife had also been invited on board to lunch as distinguished guests, but had not arrived, a message having been sent with an apology and explanation for their absence: apparently, Her Ladyship was indisposed.

Leaving the ship, and heading for home after their aforementioned, mind-blowing experiences, Archie and Margaret met their son Arthur on his rounds. He looked troubled; there was a dimming of his natural facial jollity.

It seems his 'stop-smoking' clinic of the previous week had run into difficulties due to a computer hitch. Doc. Arthur had prescribed the antismoking drug Zyban, but a malfunction by the e.Formulary I.T.system, which automatically lists the most popular drugs when G.P.'s fill out prescriptions, had led him to issue, not the nicotine cravings suppressor Zyban, but the sex stimulant Seldenafil, the generic name for which is Viagra. The male recipients of this Seldenafil had speedily lost all cravings for cigarettes, replacing them with cravings for other pleasures. Word spread, and men of all ages were turning up at the surgery asking for the blue, diamond shaped pills which were giving them a new zest for life. This popularity for giving up smoking, especially by those who were only thinking of starting to smoke, confused their locum G.P. until a deputation of wives appeared asking for sleeping pills for their husbands. One young lady explained that her mother was having sex nightly, something enjoyed in her younger days but now less so due to being eighty years of age. The popularity of the blue pills amongst the men, and unpopularity amongst the women, indicated to their temporary G.P. that something was not quite as he intended, and must be stopped immediately. Thereafter, the bedroom window lights were no longer seen to be on after midnight, and the ladies went about with less hunted expressions on their faces.

Lady Cynthia, after her previous experiences as a victim of Dr. Arthur's diagnoses and prescriptions, had already threatened her man that if he did not throw away his blue pills and start smoking again as soon as possible she would leave home (the Laird had chased her round the bushes to an alarming extent) and when he did so at her command bedroom normality was resumed. However, Archie heard whispers around the town that not all the wives welcomed the removal of the blue pills, despite their public protestations to the contrary.

Archie and Margaret, a little light-headed from the extravagance onboard the carrier, left Arthur to his problems, went home, started up their car and then drove over to Sutor House to sort out their own problems by finding out what was going on regarding the unexplained aspects of this wedding. They now fully realized there was some sort of cloak and dagger funny business going on and it was being masterminded by the evasive Veronica, but what was happening? To begin with, what was wrong with 'Sin'? Not like her to stand up an invitation from an Admiral. As they drove up to the Laird's stately home, the explanation lay before them.

A long line of pick-up trucks was spilling out a very weirdly dressed crowd of noisy people: the men wore buckskin jerkins and beaver hats, and the women sported ten gallon Stetsons, spangled waistcoats, and cowboy boots. It looked like a rally of Davy Crockets and Dolly Partons, with a few Elvis Presleys thrown in. A distraught, hand-wringing 'Sin' was watching this band of survivors from the siege of the Alamo advancing on her castle a-whooping and a-hollering. These, then, were Magdalene's 'staff', more accurately described as her multitudinous relations from the wild Allegheny Mountains of Virginia, snake handlers, hog wrestlers, and moonshine distillers from the remoter regions of our former colonies. Their cigar-smoking, pot-bellied, sunglasses-sporting grizzly bear of a leader towered over Her Ladyship, held out a horny hand and said: "Howdy, Ma'am, this sure is some swell place you've gotten here, I'm Leroy, and Ah'm sure pleased to meet you." Aghast, Cynthia fluttered like a dying swan and flew indoors. The thought that these people would be staying in her Château, and that she had turned down an admiral to await their arrival, was more than Berkshire County blood could take.

Before the unbelieving eyes of Archie and Margaret, out of the clear blue sky, an enormous Chinook helicopter descended on the front lawn. It bore the Presidential arms. Once the rotor blades stopped whirling and the dust and flying leaves had settled, out of the opening rear door of the 'copter stepped an honour guard of uniformed marines in immaculate uniforms and white gloves. These were followed by a team of heavily armed, full-metal-jacketed combat ready paratroopers who raced hither and thither to deploy a protective screen around the house. After a pause, a command was shouted from somewhere and a red carpet was rolled out; one by one the V.I.P.'s emerged to tread its plush pathway, the Admiral, the Secretary of State herself, Sheik Bin Riyadh and his harem in black burkhas, the ubiquitous Veronica, and a bevy of White House officials. The Colonel, conscious that he was not in uniform, stood before his stately home to welcome them wearing his old tweed jacket, an erect figure for his age, clear-eyed, dignified, one of those old soldiers of the Queen who never die but only fade away. Beech was quickly dispatched to bring his commander's medals; Mrs. Beech, in her best apron, curtseyed stiffly; the young housemaids lined up and sort of dipped in a giggly fashion; the great ones having descended to earth looked around to see where they had landed. The newly arrived 'good 'ole country boys and gals' watched these impressive proceedings with an initial silent awe, but speedily followed up with cries of "Hey, Hey, U.S.A." and other inane yells of the sort which our excitable transatlantic cousins disgracefully bellow out during the Ryder Cup. Television cameras appeared from the bowels of the aircraft and began to immortalize the scene.

His Lordship stood at the top of the grand stone staircase which ascended up to his stately home while his distinguished audience below gazed up at the turreted, crenellated old walls bearing the weatherworn heraldic coat of arms which proclaimed that this was the seat of an ancient and noble family, and as such should be approached with reverence. The Colonel made an impromptu speech of welcome which he based on hazy recollections of the address he had delivered the day he had welcomed General Eisenhower to the GHQ of the 51st Highland Division. In the sort of voice Americans associate with the chinless wonders of our landed gentry, he referred to his wartime service with the 'doughboys', and the special relationship of our two countries. At the same time, he took the opportunity to make reference to the several times he had been bombed in Tunisia from a great height by B17s of the U.S. Army Air force: a touchy subject, he said loftily, but he wanted it to be known that as a gentleman he was prepared to overlook these examples of gross American military ineptitude, and wished to assure his guests from our colonies in the New

World that they had nothing to fear anymore from King George III and the redcoats. So saying, he descended the steps, took Ms. Alright's hand, kissed her tenderly on both cheeks, and treated her to the sort of vulpine look which hinted that the effects of the Viagra pills on His Lordship had not entirely worn off.

Blushing somewhat, and in a higher pitched voice than normal, this famous stateswoman replied that she was delighted to be coming to visit the ancestral home of such a distinguished family as the McSutor of Sutor. A bond between her ancestors and His Lordship's clan existed through General McSutor who in 1812 had shot her great-great grandfather at the Battle of Washington and ordered the Highland Light Infantry to burn down the White House. Skipping lightly over such unhappy historical events, she noted appreciatively the present Lord Sutor's speech, and went on to express herself a great admirer of that icon of 21st century global culture, Magdalene. She had come; she informed the T.V. cameras, to this wonderful wedding to bring her President's blessing (applause). Ms. Alright then said that she had always wanted to come to Scotland, the land of Great Heart Wallace the Bruce, and those world renowned song writers, Bobby Burns and Annie Laurie. Realising she had said something unbelievably stupid, she flushed, glared at her staff and feebly laughed: "My speechwriter likes to play his little jokes on me."

"To be serious," she said, pointing up high to the statue of Alexander McTaggart on top of his column with a seagull on his head, "there stands The Pathfinder, the Scot who founded my nation and united our two peoples forever." Just when, for a moment, it seemed she might start singing The Star Spangled Banner, there was a thunderous explosion.

Everyone instinctively ducked - except for the Colonel, veteran that he was of many a bombardment by the Fritzes, and his batman Beech who, not having received any orders from his commander to take cover remained standing at attention. An R.P.G., hurtling between the Sheikh and the Secretary of State had narrowly missed them, and burst against the bastion-thick walls of Sutor House, filling the air with smoke, flying debris, and screams. Panic ensued. Ms. Alright and the Prince with his trailing harem were hastily forced to their feet by the rapid reaction force of guardian marines and bundled into the helicopter. Easy Company of the U.S. Air cavalry, ever on alert for terrorist attacks, and having taken up covering positions on arrival, began to spray the woods with automatic weapons fire. In the tremendous racket, the dazed and shell shocked Hill Billys and staff scattered, ducking and weaving everywhere except in the direction of the high ground overlooking the House from which area the rocket had come.

Amidst all the chaos and confusion, the Colonel, stood with the light of battle shining in his eyes, as composed and commanding a figure as his famous ancestor General Hector McSutor of the Royal Scots who, when his head was shot off by a cannon ball at Waterloo, coolly remarked as he fell from his old warhorse, "Mi head's gawn", and heedless and headless charged Marshall Ney's cuirassiers.

"Beech," he shouted above the din, "the blighters are shooting from mi' family graveyard on the hill. Range three hundred yards. Call out the Home Guard, Sergeant. We will set up Battalion Headquarters in the British Legion Hall immediately."

The old soldier, faithful octogenarian that he was, saluted smartly, about turned, and shuffled off to carry out his commanding officer's orders. As he did so a second R.P.G. flew at high velocity straight below the helicopter and, failing to hit its target, hurtled off to explode with a big bang in the rhubarb fields. Taking this as a strong hint to depart without further delay, the rotors started up and the giant aircraft lifted off, stirring up the surrounding turmoil and tumult to fever pitch. It rose to escape not a second too soon.

A third rocket issued from the direction of the graveyard shattering the window of the bedroom in which, at that precise moment, Her Ladyship was dressing after a restorative bath to wash off the experience of meeting Magdalene's relations. Whistling past her, the projectile holed the door, flew down the long gallery, and vacated the premises via a stained-glass window which displayed scenes of British India arranged around a portrait of Victoria Regina reigning in her imperial glory during the days of the Raj. A loud detonation indicated that the thing had exploded in the distance, leaving 'Sin' standing in her lingerie trembling and gagging on faint cries of "Help!" In such moments of stress the mind plays strange tricks, and as her husband appeared hurriedly (sad to recount, more to seek out his old military uniform and shotgun than save his beloved), she screamed: "That damned doctor tried to kill me with disease, now he is trying to blow me up!" At which point she fell upon the bed in a swoon.

The shooting paused, and was followed by increased bursts of intermittent small arms ground fire. A patrolling Apache helicopter appeared and started pouring canon rounds into the graveyard, shaking the earth, and relocating the remains of the Colonel's interred ancestors over a very wide area. Then, as quickly as it had all begun, all gunfire ceased. The graveyard was occupied by the military, but whoever they were, the terrorists (for so they must have been) had either vanished or been blown to bits. Cautiously, the shocked and dusty victims of the assault began to emerge from their hiding places and help each other to move on the run for safety in the Big House. The drivers of parked vehicles drove off at starting speeds fast enough to rival the Monte Carlo Rally.

Mrs. McTaggart, in a bedraggled and concussed state, staggered towards her car hoping to find there the protective care of her husband. He was not to be seen; she looked around but he had deserted her, disappeared. Archie's martial instincts had automatically taken him off with the attackers who had been assaulting the terrorists' position. She drove off without him, feeling much dishevelled and angered to the boiling point of what Archie called her "God Almighty Mood". When sitting behind a steering wheel in a distraught condition Margaret was not one to spare the horse power and she tore down the country road as if being launched from Cape Canaveral.

Her car was closely followed by Beech's motorbike in the sidecar of which sat the Colonel, cap back to front, wearing goggles, hooting the horn and shouting: "Clear the road for military traffic". Down into the town they helter-skeltered until the motorbike screeched to a halt outside the British Legion and Margaret, free of hot pursuit, was able to return home with tattered nerves. She had not suffered such a shattering experience since, as a rookie supply teacher, she faced her first class of unruly C stream 5th year pupils in an inner city Secondary School. The shootout at Sutor House had been almost as bad as that, which is saying something.

Beech reported: "All present and correct, Sir," as the Colonel inspected the Home Guard. These elderly gentlemen, disturbed from their afternoon dominoes, were few in number and much bemused. It was fifty years since they had last mustered, and the years had much reduced their numbers either by death, or invalidity of the flesh. The Colonel was oblivious to these facts of life, and marched them up to the Big House looking as if they were parading to a cenotaph rather than to fight against global terrorism. Leaving them panting for breath and with orders to fill sandbags, the C. in C. marched off to arm his troops from the contents of his armoury: 12-bores used when his old school tie friends from the Carlton Club came North from the metrop. for the grouse shooting. In quick time, the bunch of rejuvenated geriatrics had the House windows loop-holed for all round defense. The Colonel strode about bellowing, "Die hard, men. No confounded Wogs will frighten the British soldier." Entering into the Kiplinesque spirit of the occasion, the woodsmen from the Appalachians offered their tracking skills, and went forwards to scout for enemy activity. Sutor House had not witnessed such a scene since the Forty-Five when the Fifth Earl's militia had fought off marauding bands of ferocious, thieving Jacobite 'West Coasters' by means of homemade cannons cast by Lady Bertha McSutor in her kitchen brass foundry - Alfred Krupps named his gigantic 1914 railway gun "Big Bertha" in her memory.

Archie walked home feeling somewhat guilty at having deserted his wife at the scene of battle; he expected a hot reception. The good news he bore was that the graveyard had been captured without casualties but the bad news was that no prisoners had been taken. The terrorists had slipped away before the assault blasted their hideout out of existence. As he walked back to the manse, keeping a sharp lookout for any fugitives on the run, jet fighters from Lossiemouth zoomed and boomed overhead.

"I knew something was going on," said Archie grimly to himself. Were the rockets intended for the Sheik? Or were they aimed at the Secretary of State, that Alright dame, or both of them? Lucky they got away, and nobody else was shot up. He couldn't wait any longer before meeting Gordon and demanding to know why he had not been apprised of the fact that a war was going to break out right here in his own backyard.

As he approached the garden gate of the manse, Archie was stopped by two red-capped military policemen. They were unmoved by his salute, and insistence that he lived there and was entitled to admission. "No one is allowed in", they barked heads back to look down upon him from beneath their shiny peeked caps. "This is a state of emergency." Normally the most benign of men, Archie, aggravated beyond self-constraint, returned them a look which would have halted a stampeding horse. Eyes flashing red for danger, and a flow of language which would have made a pirate's parrot envious, were not what a redcap expects to receive from a gentleman in a clerical collar. They shifted uneasily, grew dramatically less certain of their powers of retention, and seeing that Archie's blood was up wisely let him proceed without further hindrance or comment.

There he was in the garden: Gordon, standing looking through binoculars at some object of interest on the far side of the Firth. Beside him stood Veronica holding a mobile 'phone to her ear. Archie, flushed of face, ran over to them almost bowling them over.

"What's going on?" he angrily demanded.

Gordon did not attempt to cushion the sudden impact of his old flesh and blood with a greeting and answer, instead he handed him the binoculars and pointed to a column of black smoke in the distance.

"Auchenshuggle Castle, Dad, it's on fire."

Archie looked and listened; unmistakably the sound of gunfire came from the same direction as the smoke. Well acquainted with the sound of a firefight, Archie knew a battle was raging at the Castle. After a minute's silent expert assessment of the distant contest, he turned on his heel and marched indoors shouting: "Tell those bleeding pongos to get out of my garden."

It was an uncomfortable moment for the couple he left behind, but Veronica, puzzled, managed to ask: "Gordon, what are 'pongos'? I don't know anything about 'pongos'."

Gordon, feeling bad about his father's anger, brushed her aside with: "Oh, that's just what Royal Marines call soldiers in the army - pongos. Forget it - come on."

Once indoors, it took considerable persuasion by V before Margaret agreed leave her kitchen and join her, Archie, and Gordon in the sitting room. Mum would neither speak nor look at either her husband or her son. She was furious with both of them. They almost had her killed, and she didn't understand why. Angry though she was, at the same time she was desperately curious to know what Gordon had to say about the current outbreak of violence which was frightening the life out of the whole town. For his part, acutely embarrassed, Gordon was about to offer some enlightenment as to why his parents had been shot at and come close to joining the heavenly choir, when Sylvia arrived, pushing a tea trolley and shedding tears.

"Mr. McTaggart," (Sylvia held old fashioned views on respect for a minister, even one she disliked) "my canary has passed away." She unwrapped a white cloth and showed him the pathetic wee thing which had lost its very last feather along with its last gasp and final chirp.

Everyone said: "Ah, poor wee thing," and tendered other similar expressions of sorrow as Sylvia laid the skinny mite on the table, blew her nose, sobbed some more, and poured the tea with a shaky hand. The ruse worked; with everyone sympathetic, relaxed, and rendered vulnerable, Sylvia, speaking in a quiet voice for once in her life, struck the blow: "Well, are you two going to tell us precisely what's going on, or are you not?"

As a politician, it was Gordon's practice never to answer a direct question, and he was about to temper his reply with reluctance and reservations, when Veronica stepped in to help him out. "I should have told you about a lot of things earlier," she confessed, "and I'm so, so sorry you were caught up in the unfortunate incident at the House, but there is only so much Gordon and myself know about the situation and all we can tell you is that…" Gordon put out his hand to stop her,

"Mum, Dad," he said, coming clean, "it was a set up. Auchenshuggle has been under surveillance for a long time by the international anti-terrorist secret services, MI6, C.I.A., and the French State Security. The castle was a suspected training centre for al-Qaeda. We have been carrying out covert operations there for months; they had to be flushed out before the S.A.S., could move against the place. It was more than brave of Marjorie Alright to come here as she is a prime target for Bin Laden and that's why she was exhibited at this wedding. I am not at liberty to say how these things are done, but the Islamic terrorist cells in Britain were slowly fed information that Magdalene and myself were to marry in St. Regulus and that The Secretary of State would be coming here. They took the bait, unable to resist getting massive publicity throughout the world.

The aircraft-carrier was a big draw, and we gave it maximum spin to bring out into the open terrorist sleeper cells in the big cities. We knew that a series of urban suicide bombings were being planned and we had to act to stop them."

Margaret gaped: "You mean to tell me that this gathering of the clans at Sutor House was what they call in American movies 'a stake out'? What if they had killed the Secretary of State for the U.S.A.? That could have started a war with Iran or Syria or somebody. Did you talk Alright into risking being blown to bits just so the S.A.S., or some Yankee Swot Team could have an excuse to burn down Auchenshuggle Castle?"

"And what about your mother?" chipped in Archie, taking the opportunity to get back in his wife's good books, "she could have been killed." He took her hand.

Margaret did not shrink from further indignant questioning: "What about the Sheik?" she asked, "He owns Auchenshuggle Castle so the Sheik must be one of the terrorists."

Gordon was a patient man, famous in Parliament for his prudence, tact, and self-control, virtues which misled his political colleagues and enemies into believing him to be an aloof, calculating sort of guy. His sturdy build and preoccupied facial expression made him look older than he was and did not help to dispel his reputation in Middle England as 'a dour Scot'. But outside the political mad house those who knew him well saw a different Gordon: with his mates good for a laugh; with women a charmer; with children and dogs a playmate. Still considered a young man on the up and up, he was, in fact, simply a typical University lecturer in business finance and no more 'dour' than any other of that breed of scoundrels.

"Look," said this son of the manse to his parents, "I didn't set this up - and I didn't talk Marjorie Alright into anything - she wouldn't listen to me anyway, why should she? I'm not her President and she only takes orders from him. As for the Sheikh, well what you saw was not the real Sheikh - it was his double, an impostor posing for him - they all have doubles in case of assassination attempts."

"What about his harem? Were they all doubles too?" asked his mother, still dubious.

"That's right. The Sheikh didn't mind the real ones being involved – he has lots more wives where they come from, but we insisted on hiring a troupe of exotic dancers from the *Follies Berger* to play the part. Of course, wearing burkhas you couldn't tell who or what they were, and they got good money. The Sheikh is very generous and very rich."

"I take it they were told what might happen to them - get shot," said Archie acidly, sympathetic towards the girls in black. "I hope they got plenty of danger money."

"I paid them myself - on behalf of the Sheikh, petro-dollars of course," cut in Veronica, missing Archie's sarcastic point.

Gordon leaned forwards in his chair and resumed the explanation: "The Sheikh is working for Saudi Intelligence; he hasn't been near the castle for years. He lured al-Qaeda into setting up their headquarters in the West there - it's a long, complicated story but he did it brilliantly, they never suspected a thing. We had the place bugged and our operatives knew they were on the brink of launching a big terrorist attack in London - as I said, we had to force them out of hiding so we could move in and take them all out in one single operation before some got away. I know it was high risk, but it worked - they couldn't resist shooting at Alright and the helicopter but all they did was shoot themselves in the foot, see what I mean? The gang will blow themselves up as Islamic martyrs when they realize that they can't get back to Auchenshuggle Castle and rejoin the main force. I am sure they are no longer a danger, Mum, but to reassure you, I have armed military police watching the manse - you saw them when you came home, Dad."

"I did," said his father; "Now, tell me about this high risk policy; was it decided at the top by our Prime Minister and the President? Did it cross their radar that your mother and I could have been mortally wounded visiting the Colonel? And what about all the other people there?" Archie paused, pictured 'Sin' being shot at in her negligee, enjoyed a satisfied smile, and decided to pursue this line of criticism no further.

"I, we, have told you all we can, Pop, just say that this was a vitally important operation, authorized at the very top, and carried through to a complete success. So, all I can say is thanks to you both for bearing with all the secrecy and risks. You've been great."

All this avalanche of astounding revelations took some time to sink in; the story of clandestine operations going on under their noses in sedate, peace loving St. Regulus, the garden of God's creation, was so extraordinary that even the verbal skills of Gordon, the politician par excellence, and the constraining silence of Veronica could not make what was happening believable.

Margaret sat bemused while Archie paced over to the window to look once again at the smoke on the horizon.

"Going to tell us the rest of this tale?" he said in a grating voice. "Let's see; so far the Laird has had his House, and his family burying place shelled; in rapid response, he has recalled the rheumy-eye, toothless remnants of Dad's Army to the colours and set them straining their feeble limbs to fortifying his home. A lynch mob of moccasined, bowie knife brandishing frontiersmen are wandering around the countryside like boy scouts looking for spoors so they can track down armed and highly dangerous fanatics who will happily kill them at the first chance; one of the highest classed political figures in the world has almost been assassinated before my very eyes; and a Saudi Prince of one the world's most important Sheikhdoms in Arabia, plus his harem, has been involved in an incident which could lead to war throughout the Middle East. Have I left anything out?" he asked, throwing up his hands appealingly, "if so, do tell."

Margaret got back to the harem: "Why did you hire French girls for the Sheik, or rather, the pretend Sheikh. What is wrong with our own Scots lassies? Why do we have to keep bringing in foreigners these days?"

Veronica, uncomfortable with the reference to foreigners, glanced at Gordon who nodded but was unable to think of a reply. This pleased Margaret who felt she had scored a point and demonstrated that she was not to be treated by her son as if she was a 'ga-ga' old woman.

"Who the harem girls are is irrelevant, dear," said Archie in exasperation, "the thing is that this whole business has been a sham from start to finish. How can you possibly hide it? The T.V. cameras were there and the pictures must be all over the world by now. The media are going to have a field day with this."

"They won't," said Gordon firmly; "classified information. The cameras? They were bogus - part of the deception plan. And the newspaper owners have been well warned to keep what happened at Sutor House and Auchenshuggle Castle under wraps. Of course, it is bound to come out eventually, but all the public is interested in right now is Magdalene's wedding. Don't worry, Dad, I didn't just blunder into this - the wedding gave the anti-terrorist organizations an opportunity to deal a deadly blow to Al-Qaeda and send a message to Bin Laden and his suicide bombers around the world that we are on top of security. It has been a success, urban attacks will be nipped in the bud, lives saved, and you and Mum can be proud that you assisted immensely in achieving all this. I intend seeing to it that you are both awarded the M.B.E. for something or other, charitable work or so forth, once I am P.M. Should go well with your M.C. Dad," Gordon chuckled disarmingly.

"What's in it for you?" asked Archie, knowing that behind his beloved son's smile lurked the spin doctors on his staff.

Gordon smiled more widely, knowing where his father's thoughts had led him.

"I'm not getting married tomorrow for a publicity stunt. Of course, it does do my reputation as the next P.M. a lot of good - but why not? Anyway, I am sure to be appointed soon, whether I get married or not - but being married helps with the image. Women voters like that - stability, family, that sort of thing."

Archie was not used to Gordon being so forthright, so was even more than usually suspicious: "Are you telling me this Mandolin female is really coming here, and there will be a wedding and it is going to happen the day after tomorrow?"

"Certainly," jumped in Veronica, "it truly is for real—in fact, Magdalene is already here, staying in the Royal Hotel."

"Well, you might have told us," censured Margaret in scalding tones.

Archie just breathed out in a barely audible, weary voice: "Well, I hope this Mandolin I've never seen will turn up with the Marriage Schedule, or there will be NO wedding."

"Magdalene, dear, not Mandolin - you are thinking of Captain Corelli's mandolin," corrected his wife. Turning to V she then stated sourly: "Do you think, my dear, seeing this is our family wedding in our town we might be told the names of those whom you have invited?"

Veronica, for the first time in a long time, looked disconcerted and replied apologetically: "Well, I thought it would be a great pleasure and surprise for you if, seeing you will be the First Lady at the wedding, Maggi, I invited all the ladies in your Guild." She paused for the reaction which was not long coming.

"You have what!" exploded Margaret, her jaw dropping in disbelief. "You had absolutely no right to invite anybody to our wedding - that is my responsibility and privilege."

V back-pedalled: "Of course, Maggi, how right you are, but time was running out and there is tight security to consider, so I had to restrict the guest list to approved individuals and groups. As for the Marriage Schedule papers, that has all been fixed at the Registry Office; everything is in order."

"Damn your security and your 'in order'," swore the Lady of the Manse, startling everyone. There was a very embarrassing silence. Archie was struck dumb; he had never heard Margaret swear, though he had often enough heard her reproving him for doing so. It was plain she was deeply annoyed. She rose to her feet. So did Veronica to offer mollifying words.

"Maggi, I do hope you will forgive me for being hasty and forward. Please, give your approval for this. It means so much to the Guild ladies. I have arranged three buses to take them into Inverness to buy new clothes for the wedding - at our expense, of course. They didn't mind one little bit. They left this morning - should return this evening. I do hope that was all right with you? I told them it was your idea. I meant to tell you earlier but all the trouble at Sutor House...and well...everything else... "

Margaret now realised why all her many Guild ladies' telephone calls to the manse had abruptly ceased. Her nerves had cracked under all the pressure of events for a few hours, but her resilient intelligence, resourcefulness, and experience gained from a life dealing with pupils and people had made her well equipped to see opportunities in the shocks that flesh is heir to. Though having her Guild ladies invited *en masse to* the wedding by someone other than herself did not appeal, being credited with the idea of them being subsidised on a massive scale to go on a free shopping spree would stand her reputation in very good stead for years to come, and furthermore, she could charge her own expensive outfit to V - something that would please her husband no end.

As women always do, in that mysterious way men can never understand, Margaret, swiftly swung from confrontation to sisterly affection, and she led V off into the kitchen (where all the real business gets done in a family) so that, in mutual delight and satisfaction, they could plan the arrangements for the great day - church, reception, the lot.

Sylvia drifted in tearfully still carrying the canary. She took the mortal remains of the deceased warbler, such as they were, into the garden for burial. "Bury yourself with it, you old bag," muttered Archie, lapsing from Christian charity into peevishness. Will Rogers, the American humorist famous for his homespun philosophy

144

and cracker-barrel wit, once claimed he had never met anyone he disliked, an admirable sentiment, indeed, but one which Archie put down to the great Will never having met Sylvia.

Time for man-to-man talk: "You going to get married tomorrow, Gordon?"

"Yes, that's right Dad."

"No more 'surprises' to upset your mother?"

"She will be delighted."

"And she's here, Magdalene - in the Crown?"

"With her security people; we put the media off the scent by leaking the story that she would be staying at Auchenshuggle, but, obviously, she couldn't go there. The great thing is that the paparazzi have all gone over there for the action and left her in peace."

"They got plenty of action, all right. Did you know that in the 'Twenties and 'Thirties Auchenshuggle Castle had quite a reputation for *hanky-panky* - the previous owner was the Duchess of Ross, one of the Bloomsbury set, free love and all that. They were all at it, bed hopping, wife-swopping, sex parties - the locals called it 'Bouncy Castle'. By the way, what was all this about attempts on Magdalene's, life in the past?"

"Oh, those were in the States, not here. Thing is, celebrities and politicians expect that sort of thing. I have my own bodyguard, you know, you won't see him but he is always there. Magdalene and I must always take precautions. You just never know."

Archie felt some more things needed clearing up, so he said in fatherly tones: "Veronica, you know her, don't you, Gordon."

"Very well, we have met many times here and over the pond. She is Magdalene's agent - but you know already know that."

Archie was no fool: "Do you trust her, Gordon? You seem to be fond of her, and she seems fond of you."

"Of course, Veronica is highly efficient, classy. Magdalene is going to miss her."

"Why? Is she leaving her job soon?"

"So she says. You know Dad how sometimes when you are driving along and every red light ahead turns to green at exactly the right moment; well it's been like that for me lately. You know how long I have waited for the P.M's job and I want you both to be proud of me, you and Mum. I can't wait to see you coming into Number 10, everybody outside waving and cheering."

Gordon was waxing lyrical but Archie did not fail to notice he had changed the subject. He did the same himself, trying a new tack.

"She is friendly with the Marquis, isn't she? You know him?"

"No, never met him."

Archie pressed the questioning: "But you know what he is doing here, don't you? And that Veronica knew him before she came here."

Gordon shuffled uneasily in his chair before coming out with it: "He is working for French Intelligence. Our own Secret Service has known for some time that Mossad has also had him watching Auchenshuggle Castle for Jewish Intelligence. As for Veronica, she is with the C.I.A."

Way beyond surprises, Archie nodded an 'I knew it all along' nod as if he really had known it all along which he had not. So that was it. And that was why he had all that radio equipment in his attic - radio buff, my arse.

"He really is French; I believe he spent a lot of his time in French speaking Canada," further divulged Gordon.

"But he's not really a Marquis?"

"Well, he really could be, you never know with these guys. He's not an assassin like The Jackal or anyone like that. And he really is in show business and Hollywood films and that sort of thing as well as working for the *Surete* people in Paris. Talented man."

"He fairly gets about - so, he knows Magdalene, then?"

"Very, very well, I'm told. Through entertainment - Los Angeles, Atlantic City, concerts all over the world."

After his spell of plain talking, Gordon reverted to speaking in sound bites. Nevertheless, for Archie some of the pieces of this bizarre tale were falling into place and, he began to get the picture. Being initiated into Gordon's lunatic world of espionage did not make him feel superior to others (he was already superior being a Marine) but it did make him feel an 'insider', one of the elect, a *bona fide* plotter. This was gratifying but at the same time something still bothered Archie: it was the nagging suspicion that he had not been told everything and that there were things that Gordon was hiding. He couldn't be sure that every one of these terrorists had been eliminated. What if one or two were still at large?

He was too tired to ride any longer on this clandestine merry-go-round; get the wedding over, then back to normal and the sooner the better. He had not the least desire to visit Number 10, or the Houses of Parliament. Politics held no interest for him, and, as the hymn says, "Fame is transitory, riches fade away," the sooner his incoming daughter-in-law faded away as well, the better.

Archie knew his son too well to be completely taken in by a politician, and Gordon knew his father too well not to know that he was none too happy at the way he had been deceived. Archie looked tired; he sat hunched up, his face as mournful looking as a terminally ill parson called upon to dedicate a new mortuary. Gordon felt bad about that; he revered his father, saw him as the finest Christian man he had known. Something nice needed to be said to cheer Pop up.

"Arthur is best man, Dad. You'll know that. Great isn't it?"

Archie sparked again: "Where is Arthur? Been gone all day. Not another Hepatitis pandemic, I hope?"

Gordon laughed knowing the story of the hepatitis outbreak. Archie smiled wryly.

"Last Veronica and I saw of him, he was going into the Post Office with books for Katie to take back to the library."

"Aye, that'll be the third time this week he's taken books back. Katie isn't working for the C.I.A. as well, I hope."

"No, relax Pop, she is just our Katie. Why a good looking and brilliantly clever lass like her, with all those degrees, runs a Post Office and an evening library and hasn't been snapped up as a wife I can't understand. She's a cracker, and only twenty-six. By the way, did I tell you, Katie is partnering Arthur - she will be the best maid? He asked for her especially so that Katie can lead in Magdalene's sisters, the bridesmaids."

Archie sensed a message coming through somewhere. He would ask Margaret what it was. She had always had local knowledge about people when he knew nothing about them and their doings.

Gordon went off during the evening meal to answer his secure telephone line (presumably to talk to his bride to be), leaving the company at table enjoying good humoured conversation which did not dwell upon the day's events. Archie mischievously started pulling Arthur's leg about seeing a lot of Katie; this caused Margaret to swiftly redirect the conversation to Veronica requesting that the wedding invitations to Guild members did not include Cynthia. If she came, then let be it under her own banner.

Margaret was in scintillating form doing her 'hostess with the mostess' act to perfection. Later in the evening, she was in even higher spirits following a telephone call from Sutor House by none other than Her Ladyship asking where in the kirk she and the Laird would be seated. Margaret had never heard her so meek and mild and humble, the poor woman sounded battle fatigued after her day of humiliation and distress. This was a different double-barrelled Lady Cynthia Buckingham-McSutor than the one with whom Margaret had had long wrestled for supremacy. Too good a person to exult in the downfall of an opponent, Margaret answered, gently and kindly, that she and her husband had reserved a special place in the Laird's loft for their accommodation. 'Sin' sounded truly grateful (presumably for not being seated with the Hill Billies who were holding a cacophonous barn dance in the Great Hall as she spoke), so Margaret could afford to be magnanimous, knowing she had won a minor victory. Of course, it would not be long before Her Ladyship got up steam again, but for the moment, Margaret was up on points, and much pleased about it.

It was in this happy frame of mind that she accompanied Archie upstairs to their bedroom, and her joy was complete when she showed him her new dress - a designer creation carefully chosen to guarantee that no other lady would be wearing the same item at the wedding. As Charles Lamb astutely observed, no woman, be she eighteen or eighty ever dressed at less than her best, and

Margaret wanted to look her best. She was as excited about this wedding as she had been about her own as a young bride in Kirkwall Cathedral.

On that memorable day, her agitated nervous condition had not been helped by Archie deciding to take his dog for a long walk an hour before the church service; with Margaret chomping on the bit, he had to be searched out and reminded that his presence was required most urgently. As a wife, whenever she detected similar lapses in Archie's attention span, as she often did from time to time down the passing years, Margaret was quick to remind him that she had not forgotten his dog-walking disappearance on the happiest day of a girl's life. His peevish defence to this was that she had made a big fuss about nothing; he would have arrived at the church in plenty of time, no bother. If there was one thing Archie could not abide it was making a fuss about nothing; it really riled him. Margaret took a very different view, especially with regard to weddings.

The memory of her wedding day long ago came back vividly to Margaret as she lay getting her treasured cuddles in Archie's arms and she relived it once again. For his part, he was on the point of silently slipping into sleep when she began her pillow-talk: "Archie," she whispered, "you asleep?" He grunted. Why did she always want to talk when he wanted to sleep? One of the trials of married life, he had discovered. Margaret was still talking about how he had taken the dog for a walk an hour before their wedding when he began to snore like an asthmatic hippopotamus. Archie's snoring was one of the trials of married life for Margaret, so they evened out.

That night Arthur slipped out of the manse very late.

CHAPTER ELEVEN

The Great Day

The morning came bright but blustery, a strong, wind pushing against the west facing side of the wee town. This left the east side sheltered and it was there that the crowds were already gathering around the kirk for the wedding, milling excitedly around a massive television van. By now, the news that the future Prime Minister was about to marry the most famous female performer in the popular music celebrity scene had set the entire civilized and semi-civilized world agog. With Magdalene the wife of the British P.M. and living in Downing Street, it would be 'Cool Britannia' right enough!

What mystified the principalities and powers who owned and ran the world's media was that the marriage had been so successfully kept secret in these days of I.T. with its coverage of everything and anything. One of the top range magazines had paid a huge sum for exclusive rights to cover the wedding but that did not satisfactorily explain why the lid had been put on information; the newshounds from the press knew full well that the wedding, the battle of Sutor House, and the assault on Auchenshuggle Castle must be somehow connected, and they were desperate to find out how.

Margaret and her mother went to the church early to help the Guild ladies decorate the pews and aisles with garlands, and arrange the magnificent display of flowers. The ladies were in their element, dressed to the nines, busy, laughing.

She returned to find Archie hovering around the manse strictly banned from taking the dog a walk to pass the waiting time. This displeased his dear wee 'Pepsi' who, deprived of the highlight of her day, sulked in her basket, while Alfie, the cat, who always accompanied the two of them on their walks, stuck his tail up to show he was cheesed off. Archie tried to reason with them: a cat can go for a walk any time without following man and dog, he told Alfie, pointing to the open backdoor, but his feline friend was unimpressed and disdainfully high tailed it as cat's do when offended.

With time on their hands, Margaret turned her thoughts to the reception and Archie's limitations as a dancer. A wife has been defined as 'a woman who thinks that her husband does not dance enough', and Margaret, a devotee of 'Strictly Come Dancing' on T.V., longed to dance away the night at the reception. Archie had become adequate, if not proficient, at the waltz and quick-step but needed training in the fox-trot. So, with time on her hands, she worked his stumbling feet at this movement. Outside in the garden, Arthur paced up and down anxiously fingering the rings and rehearsing his lines, the wind blowing his kilt in an eye-catching fashion. A first-timer, a novice at making speeches, Arthur dreaded the reception as do all poor suckers dragooned into being Best Man.

Gordon was in pinstripes, and tails, looking like a Japanese statesman (a tall Japanese statesman). He reckoned that wearing a kilt would not go down well with the English voters in the Home Counties, and for a politician votes are what life is about. He was not in the least nervous, for bridegrooms never are, and filled in the waiting time by reading the contents of his ministerial dispatch box.

Katie was as excited as a school girl getting seven A-grades in her Highers; she had sat up very late, and hardly slept, but appeared much the better for it. When the car arrived to take her to the kirk, she looked stunningly beautiful, so much so that the bride faced stiff competition for centre stage.

These badly behaved days, wedding guests arrive whenever they feel like turning up; grinning vacantly, they push past the bride in the porch ready to make her grand entrance. Such misconduct was not on at this wedding. You had to come early to get your seat.

The old kirk, the first post-Reformation place of worship built in Scotland, was without a nave, being 'T' shaped with pews to the right side, left side, and in front of the central pulpit which was backed against the wall behind the small Communion Table. Lofts, (Laird's loft to the right, Scholar's loft to the left, Public loft straight ahead) extended over the lower floor-level pews allowing a headroom of only some twelve feet. The wee kirk was severely cramped for space on big occasions. Plain pine wood, white washed plaster walls adorned by a few memorial tablets for the fallen, it was a country church and, though now lit by electricity, the old oil lamps still hung there, pegs once used to hang bunnets and stovepipe hats stuck out of the overhead beams, and there were rings in the aisles for shepherds to tie up their dogs during worship. The simplicity of this House of God gave it an intimate and informal yet truly venerable atmosphere.

Timing their arrival so as to be noticed coming in, the Laird and Lady Cynthia enthroned themselves in the Laird's loft, second row. Sylvia and Margaret sat in the front row, centre, occupying pride of place and enjoying the best view of the spot where the vow swopping business was to be done. Beside and around them sat the Sheikh and his harem, prominent guests who excited considerable attention in the congregation. Beforehand, Archie had ascertained that this really was the genuine Sheikh, not a double; and the ladies of the harem in their

153

black burkhas were also the real article - which was disappointing for Archie who had been looking forward to meeting the girls from the *Folies Bergere*. The pews beneath the Laird's loft were crammed with gorgeously apparelled Guildswomen exuding romantic wedding fever and feeling younger than they had for many moons. For once, they had no interest in the whereabouts of their husbands.

The Admiral and his officers, surrounded by gum-chewing mountain men and their 'squaws', occupied the scholar's loft, which creaked alarmingly under the strain of bearing an unusually heavy load of passengers. Beneath sat Magdalene's 'heavies' from the hotel – C.I.A., F.B.I. and other official and unofficial representatives of organized crime in America. The Secretary of State, Ms. Alright, remained on board ship by command of the President acting on the precautionary advice of his counter-terrorist watchdogs at the Pentagon. The rest of the wee kirk was filled with local notables who had been admitted by armed police after showing I.D., and submitting to a body search.

Archie, Gordon, and Arthur turned up, pushed their way through the cheering crowd packing the street (children at the front waving Union Jacks and the Stars & Stripes), and past the T.V. cameramen and photographers standing on ladders and walls straining for a good view. The pair of them gained entrance into the 'hole-in-wa" sized vestry and settled down to await the bride.

It was Archie's custom, as the officiating officer during these anticipatory times of high tension, to provide the bridegroom with a yo-yo. Archie had read that the Duke of Wellington, on the eve of battle, composed himself for the fray by playing with a yo-yo, and he reckoned that what had worked at Waterloo would work equally well on the eve of a wedding. While Gordon took his mind off the walk to the scaffold by trying to make

Archie's yo-yo do what yo-yos are supposed to do, Arthur hopped about as if bursting for the toilet, rolling his eyes, twisting his fingers, and fiddling in his pockets checking he had the ring.

The sound of the bagpipes wheezing into the stirring tune of 'The 93rd's Advance on Sebastopol' indicated the arrival of the bride in her limousine. Archie posted Gordon and Arthur before the Communion Table, and went to the front door where stood Beech in full Highland dress, resplendent in pipe major's uniform, an impressive sight, or it would have been impressive had it not been for a large, stray, black Labrador, which had taken the opportunity to accompany the piping of Beech by 'singing' as dogs do. The combined musical effect of wind bag, pipe reeds, and canine vocal chords is doubtless entertaining to a pack of hungry wolves, but not to the human ear. The hills were alive with the sound of an eerie canine howling which, though in the right key, was not in keeping with Beech's performance or the occasion. The sound of the bagpipes appeals greatly to a doggie's ear so, at full volume, the songster gave his all to the performance while the piper was giving his all to removing the unwanted vocalist. Playing the pipes while side-footing away man's best friend takes some doing, and each time Beech succeeded in chasing the beastie, it returned to sit at his side, throw back its head, and open up where it left off. The onlookers were very much amused by these tussles between happy dog and exasperated bagpiper (there were mocking cries of: "Give us 'Daddy Wouldn't Buy Me A Bow Wow", and the like with much laughter. Beech admitted defeat, gave up, saluted and marched off followed off stage by the tyke which had stolen the show.

Attention turned to the arriving bride in a wedding dress so expensive and so…well so…well so out-of-this-world gorgeous that several of the ladies in the "oohing" and "aahing" crowd felt dizzy and faint. Archie formed the wedding party up to make their grand entrance: bride on the gentleman's arm, Katie behind, bridesmaids leading the toddling Sunday school flower girls by the hand, Darlene in clerical-collar and billowing multi-coloured robes bringing up the rear. A hush descended upon the awestruck spectators.

There was no time for any but the briefest introductions and chummy welcomes, but from a swift once-over, Archie guessed, correctly, that the top-hatted figure before him was no backwoods 'Pappy'; whoever he was, he was obviously a man accustomed to wealth and a high social standing.

Tall, this look-alike for Woodrow Wilson (pince-nez and all) glad-handed Archie and spoke, in an accent reminiscent of Alistair Cook's 'Letter from America', saying: "Jim, I believe we have met before, Sir...Harvard Law School versus Edinburgh University Divinity Faculty, 1962, the Old Course, St. Andrews."

Archie remembered him; a skinny youth of moderate golfing talent...but time was pressing: "Catch up later, great to see you again, Jim - mustn't keep the bridegroom waiting." In the porch, he put the bride on the Woodrow Wilson's right arm, and after checking out her dress and posture, fragrant bouquet at the ready, Archie signalled to Miss Campbell, the organist, to play them in with Mendelssohn's Wedding March. Off went the column down the short aisle in stately fashion, the bride in dazzling white satin, her face veiled in finest lace.

They made a lovely couple, standing there side by side, confident, happy, made for each other. The guests could not restrain their admiration and loud murmurs rippled round the ancient walls. A sob or two came from the ladies present, and eyes were dabbed to mop up tears of joy. Then, a solemn hush fell over all; Archie coughed and opened up with a short prayer.

In his ministry, Archie was well-known and much appreciated for the brevity of his prayers. Many an aged parishioner on his deathbed had whispered with his dying breath, "Get McTaggart for the funeral, he will be short." And Archie was short: the 23rd Psalm, a few words commending the soul to the Lord, then off to the Co-op Hall for steak pie and a beer. At the crematorium, Archie allowed no lengthy tributes, no encores, no second curtain calls; it was in and out quick. To show appreciation for these pacey performances, Archie had been voted the title *The Crème de la Crem'* by the 'Confederation of Undertakers, U.K.', and given a standing ovation at their annual dinner. As for the deceased, unable to show their approval directly, these looked down from heaven thankful that Archie had not kept them waiting on a slow gas. It is this sort of encouraging feedback which guides a minister into a better understanding of the blessings brevity bestows on a congregation, and probably the Almighty too, for His ears, ever open to the prayers of the humble, must be grateful when they keep it short.

The wedding ceremony moves from the opening prayer to a solemn admonition from the minister on the duties marriage imposes: 'marriage should not be entered upon lightly, or unadvisedly, but thoughtfully, reverently, and in the fear of God etc.". Bridegrooms receive the reading of this passage from the book with hanging heads, they clutch their trouser legs like a drowning man clutching at straws; there he stands, in his hired suit, transfixed, looking like a man getting sixty days in the Sheriff Court for something he hasn't done. The bride, close to tears, tries to shyly smile in a vain effort to soften the minister's stern looks.

Looking stern did not come easily to Archie on this occasion for the lined up buxom country gal bridesmaids before him were wearing what are called 'see-through blouses', transparent garments which expose more of a comely young lady than any red-blooded male can be expected to find uninteresting. So Archie's eyes wandered periodically (involuntarily one must say for the sake of his reputation) from the Book of Common Order to the bridesmaids, but with admirable self-control, he managed to stick somehow to reading, eyes down, the text in his hands.

The earnest "I require and charge you both, as you shall answer on the Day of Judgment" bit over, that brings the Service to; "Wherefore if anyone can show any just cause why they may not be lawfully joined together in marriage, let him now declare it."

It was at this point that the most memorable event in the long history of St. Regulus' kirk took place, never to be forgotten.

A sudden commotion drew every eye to the Laird's loft. One of the Sheikh's harem broke ranks, jumped out of the pew, tore off the smothering, all-enveloping black garment and revealed not a woman but a man wearing a grey and yellow soldier's uniform. Small, bearded, agitated about something, he produced a flag bigger than himself and began waving it about. The American sailors present, and Magdalene's relatives, instantly identified this as the flag of the Army of the Southern Confederacy (white stars along the arms of a blue X cross on a bright red background) and members of the congregation familiar with 'Gone with the Wind' speedily came to the same conclusion. Before startled eyes, this unknown warrior

158

climbed up on the balcony rail of the loft swaying precariously, swinging his banner, yelping the blood-curdling Rebel Yell and shouting in his Southern accent: 'Death to damned Yankees'. Drawing a huge revolver he aimed it at those members of the O'Hara clan visible to his line of fire. In so doing, this fanatic gave notice that the O'Hare v. O'Hara feud was still under warranty, and that the O'Hares had not forgotten the Civil War sympathies of the pro-Union O'Haras, nor the 'shotgun wedding' of one of their kinsmen to fifteen year old Annie O'Hara, alias Magdalene, when her brother, in church, had shot dead the bridegroom with a shotgun.

Being short-sighted, and having come without his spectacles to help focus upon the target, 'Johnny Reb.' leaned forwards from his perch, balanced there unsteadily, and with a shaky hand drew a bead on the O'Hara pews below. Gaping upwards at this incredible sight, the congregation sat in paralyzed silence; no one stirred a muscle or blinked an eyelid - except that is for Sylvia. This feisty lady, who was strategically seated behind the assailant, jumped up from her seat, stuck out her umbrella and poked him firmly in the back. He staggered, lost his balance, caught his spurs in the folds of the flag, dropped the revolver and followed it all the way down to the floor below where his fall was providentially broken by landing on the soft, ample bosom of Darlene. Scrambling to his feet, he clutched at the bride's dress, tearing off her veil, and escaped through a side door, limping off on a sprained ankle. In an instant, Magdalene's bodyguards drew their 'pieces' and went after him, leaving behind a scene of confusion and commotion.

Having been under fire in assorted war zones, Archie kept his cool and signalled to Miss Campbell to start playing something on the organ while he restored order. This diminutive Glasgow lady's organ playing may have left much to be desired, but in composure and courage she lacked nothing and was up to meeting the present crisis situation for she had seen worse communal upheavals on her travels. On holiday in Los Angeles during the Watts riots, while armed gangs looted stores in burning streets, she responded to an armed policeman's concern for her safety by saying 'It's all right, officer, I'm used to this. I am a Secondary School teacher from Glasgow.' So it was that, without a trembling hand, Miss Campbell rallied the congregation by playing "Nearer My God to Thee", and to those melancholy strains, reminiscent of the sinking of the Titanic, things started to settle down.

To further restore order out of chaos, Archie decided to announce the uplifting of an offering and everyone began searching through their pockets for loose change. As the elders went round with the plates, Archie took the opportunity to look around the kirk, and that is when he got the shock of his life: the unveiled bride before him giving the kiss of life to the prostrate Darlene was none other than Veronica!

He stood there totally unable to speak, unsure whether to be angry or what to say. So he adopted the "Now then, what's all this then?" policeman approach which he used whenever caught out. It worked, as usual, and Archie 'arrested' the wedding party, taking them off into the vestry. Crowded in, the inquest began while the bridesmaids wept buckets, and the bride's mother, who had appeared from nowhere, threatened to strangle the bridegroom for exposing her child to grave danger. After removing all those present who were surplus to requirements, Archie demanded silence and started his quest for answers to what had happened by asking Veronica grimly: "Well, what's the ruddy game?"

Veronica's father was asking himself the same question-plainly, he had had no idea that the wedding was for somebody else and not intended for his daughter. The situation did not bring tidings of great joy to his paternal heart, and a look as black as the Earl of Hell's waistcoat showed that he felt about Gordon the way Moses felt about the Amalakites. It goes without saying that having his little girl shot at by some maniac on the happiest day of her life does not go down well with a doting father (if it goes without saying why say it? Because, dear reader, I have married off daughters myself and know the feeling, okay?)

"Dad," said Gordon, addressing his Dad-to-be, "Veronica and I are truly sorry. We never expected this. Magdalene wanted so much to have a quiet wedding, away from the media, so we misled them into coming here. We didn't have a chance to tell you." Turning to Archie he carried on with his placatory mission saying: "Veronica intended taking off her veil just before the vows so you got the names right. We thought you knew. Didn't Mum tell you? She knew all about it. You weren't supposed to be surprised at all."

Archie received this bombshell with impressive aplomb for he knew what would ensue when he targeted Margaret in his sights: he would angrily denounce her for not telling him something that it was blindingly obvious it was essential for him to know; she would return his serve by accusing of making a drama about nothing and reminding him that he needed to get his ears syringed and the wax removed. He would fume at this *non sequitur* but she would loftily retort that it had merely slipped her mind to tell him and anyway he never listened to anything she said, and she probably did tell him after all so it was entirely his fault. No woman in history having ever been wrong, she would leave Archie without room in his mind for doubt on that score.

It was at this fraught juncture, that Margaret materialized in their midst wearing a smile as big as her hat and shining with happiness - to her immense relief her beloved boy was not marrying Magdalene after all. Instead, he was one-fleshing himself with the admirable Veronica, a woman she held in high esteem, born of good stock, a worthy P.M's wife-to-be, the daughter she had always wanted but which the Lord had denied her for inscrutable reasons of His own.

Archie capitulated; lifting hands and eyes to heaven he gave her the plaintive Oliver Hardy "Here's another fine mess you've gotten me into Stanley" look. This did not take away her smiles so he plodded on: "I take it you have the marriage schedule and it is all in order?" he asked Best Man Arthur. Katie, still clutching her bouquet, nodded vigorously on his behalf, and putting the words into his mouth so she could take them out again added, "Arthur has Veronica's wedding ring as well." To prove her point, she delved into his jacket pocket and produced the evidence, Arthur submitting meekly to her take over bid.

Miss Campbell was running out of music when they returned to look for Darlene and inquire solicitously if she had suffered any injuries. Apart from having the breath knocked out her she was as good as new but, fearing a second assault from the air, decided to cut short her part in the ceremony and keep her poetic contribution for another day and another wedding.

Order restored, normal service was resumed: the wedding party lined up before the altar, and Archie offered apologies to the congregation for the disruption which had taken place together with an assurance that there would be no further threats to their safety and well-being. In a brief survey of recent past events he told the agitated O'Hara clan that, although he had no idea where she was, everything was being done for the safety of Magdalene, their flesh and blood and prized source of their income.

The Colonel, unconvinced that the crisis was over, rose from his seat to read out his grandfather's grubby copy of The Riot Act, declare a state of emergency, impose martial law, and post his Home Guardsmen at the doors. On seeing this intention to carry out what they called 'kick ass', the militant wing of the O'Haras burst into warm applause, gave the bride and groom many 'high-fives', danced about a good deal, and began singing, unaccompanied, the only hymn they knew: 'Shall We Gather at the River'.

For the second time, Veronica (unveiled) and Gordon appeared before the altar. Margaret choked up, the ladies of the Guild were in seventh heaven, rings exchanged kissing of the bride took its natural course. They were man and wife. At their exit into the bright sunshine and confetti casting, Beech piped out the happy couple by playing 'Marie's Wedding'. In the far distance the banished Labrador, frustrated but not silenced, could be faintly heard joining in the libretto.

Gordon threw silver coins to the scrambling children, and Veronica threw her bouquet to an appreciative Katie. Off they went, presumably to the Crown Hotel for the reception.

Dispatches from Magdalene's private army began filtering back to the kirk, reporting that their quarry, the erstwhile fleeing gunman, had escaped on horseback. Bloodhounds were following his trail and it was believed he had lost his way and holed up in a barn. The O'Haras, who knew the culprit well, gave his name as John Wilkes Booth O'Hare Jnr., a 'good ole country boy' and fully paid up member of the Ku Klux Klan. The Colonel, in need of reinforcements, deputised all the O'Haras of military age to replace several nonagenarian Home Guardsmen who were so slow moving that a glacier would have raced past them. A posse took off for the barn.

Archie, seeing that this theatrically inclined would-be assassin from Dixie had made a significant, if indirect, contribution to his wife's happiness, and had, after all, done no actual harm to anyone, personally pleaded with beefy Leroy, Chief of the O'Hara tribe, to restrain his warriors on the war path and order them to show clemency when (or if) the O'Hare scoundrel gave himself up. In other words, lynching was out. Moved by Archie's words of goodwill towards men, Leroy came close to agreeing with him - close, but not close enough. Fortunately for the miscreant, he surrendered in time to avoid the rope, and wailing about his ankle, was taken into custody by the polis.

Her husband insisting on giving her an armed escort, Her Ladyship was driven home lying down on the back seat for safety, a broken woman, raving about rockets in the bedroom, and mad gangsters in the church. Broadcasting that she was feeling desperately ill, she called for a doctor, any doctor, provided it was definitely NOT Dr. Arthur McTaggart. Cursing his name and reputation, she swore that that 'quack' would never again come anywhere near her bedside.

After counting his harem to make sure he had no more than the normal allocation of wives and concubines, the Sheikh swept off in his magnificent attire and gleaming Rolls Royce. He made for a gathering of folk meeting at the lighthouse on the rocky peninsula beside the harbour. The Sheikh knew where he was going, and Archie soon found out why. Magdalene and the Marquis were there.

CHAPTER TWELVE

The Wind of Change

To describe what happened next is to test the credulity of readers to the limits, but fact is, after all, 'stranger than fiction', and that's a fact.

A letter from Magdalene arrived by courier at the half emptied kirk asking Archie to come to the lighthouse where she intended marrying the Marquis with his ministerial blessing and co-operation. She had attached her intended's C.V. for Archie's enlightenment, and reassurance that his credit as a potential bridegroom was good with the Lord. She did not include any information about herself because it was her unquestioned assumption that Archie, together with all the rest of mankind, already knew her life story from beginning to so far...

The Marquis' C.V. made very, very, VERY interesting reading: he was Magdalene's hitherto unnamed second husband, the one whose marriage to her had been annulled by the Pope on the grounds that she was an unshriven Baptist when they didn't get wed – or did get wed, take your pick. As for the two children, Francis was adopted but Collete was not: she was Magdalene's own child fathered by the Marquis. This was the biggest secret of all time, kept even from Veronica who otherwise knew everything about Magdalene and the Marquis. What did emerge from this mind-boggling review was that he really was involved in the movie/show business industry in the States; and he really was a French Secret Service spy, working for all sorts of secret service agencies including (this was a new one) Egyptian Intelligence. He had been sent to St. Regulus to keep an eye on Auchenshuggle Castle on behalf of the anti-terrorist branch of MI5 because it was on British soil. He had, of course, not told Magdalene that Veronica was a C.I.A. agent. It all sounded very complex, as these matters in the murky world of espionage inevitable do, but if the British Government knew all this then, of course, so did Gordon too.

"Well, well," smiled Archie, "Veronica eh! She really is a spy, a Mata Hari, *femme fatale* and all that - you never know who you are talking to." He sniffed and read on...

Henri, as Magdalene now called him in the letter, was the only man she truly loved, and they both found that they couldn't live without each other. The Pope having shown reluctance to annul the annulment they had decided to annul it themselves and remarry, this time with *nihil obstat* for good measure. As the Marquis was in St. Regulus and by happy coincidence Gordon came from there and the name St. Regulus had a classic, five-star ring to it they had decided it was a fantastically romantic spot for a wedding (she must have been breathlessly excited when she wrote that bit, thought Archie). He could see that she really had the hots for Henri. The papers, she reported, were all in order, checked out by the Registrar. She and Henri were under starter's orders at the lighthouse, just waiting for Archie to oblige and shout 'Go'.

Having been warned by Veronica that 'Scotch' ministers are not up for rental, like cars in the States, Magdalene diplomatically anticipated his caveat about them choosing the lighthouse instead of the church for the ceremony. On page two, she explained that they wanted to be rejoined together in holy wedlock on the rocks because that was where, figuratively speaking, their marriage had ended up in the first place. (Archie could see that symbolism was heavily involved here. If that is what she

167

wants, then so be it, he thought resignedly - brides always get their own way).

The letter lengthened, interesting Archie considerably: by way of explaining the secrecy of all the above, he gathered that Henri was living under a death threat, a fatwa issued against him for his activities in Algeria on behalf of French intelligence. Keeping the wedding venue secret till the last possible moment had been essential. The lighthouse with its wide open spaces all around was the ideal spot for security and their becoming, once again, man and wife. Besides, a certain magazine had bought exclusive rights to the wedding pictures for millions of dollars and that would keep away the clamouring media wolves. The magazine would be taking photographs, but assuredly not during the ceremony (too true they won't thought Archie). Everything would be proper and discreet. The letter concluded by inviting Rev. McTaggart to pray for them and come with his lovely wife to the lighthouse as soon as convenient - i.e. right now.

Archie passed word round to everyone to follow him, and set off for the nearby venue accompanied by a jocund company of Guild ladies and others. Gordon and his bonny bride had departed for an undisclosed destination; The Crown? Wedding reception? Honeymoon? Archie was past caring. He was much relieved that at long last he was looking down the eighteenth fairway, the flag was in sight, only one wedding to go and he could hand in his score card.

The rocky promontory on which the lighthouse stood had one major drawback: it was the windiest spot in St. Regulus and Daft Willie had forecast high winds. As the wedding guests walked along the path from the harbour to the stubby lighthouse with its low courtyard wall, what had been, at the eastern end of town, just a fresh wind had became a strong Westerly, blustering into gusts of alarming force. Holding on to their hats, the ladies filed along the narrow track into such shelter as was offered by the courtyard wall, cowering low there as they battled the elements.

The lighthouse had been easily sealed off by Magdalene's security gorillas and was mercifully bereft of media photographers. Out in the Firth, yachts sped by enjoying the wild winds, their owners clinging to the masts, some trying to look towards the lighthouse through binoculars, others struggling to stand upright to take pictures. Even the deck of the USS Olympia, lined with sailors staring ashore, rolled in the troubled waters. This was not a good day for an outdoor wedding at the lighthouse on the rocks.

The Marquis arrived wearing the gold-braided uniform and medals of a high ranking gendarme, looking as dapper as Claude Raines in the closing scenes of 'Casablanca'. Gone was the easy going, denim-clad Canadian *ami* with whom Archie had buddied up; here was an official, a man of authority, the sort of fastidious Frenchman who wastes no time before issuing orders.

Being well acquainted with the updraughts, downdraughts, headwinds, tailwinds, and junior hurricanes which oft assail the lighthouse, and having just passed Daft Willie with the whirligig on his helmet spinning fast enough to provide the town with electricity, Archie strongly advised the bridegroom not to hold the ceremony on the rocks but in the courtyard, inadequate though that area was for protection from the stormy blast. Disregarding this wise counsel, the Marquis ordered that a folding table be placed on the rocks just out of reach of the waves, and when this flimsy object immediately blew away he replaced it with another, this time weighing it

169

down with stones. Archie began to wonder how he had ever seen any good in this jumped up Froggie aristocrat whose ancestors he now realised had had their heads guillotined off for very good reasons.

Magdalene arrived on her father Leroy's arm, and even Solomon, in all his glory, was not arrayed as she was that day. Her daffodil yellow dress had been designed and tailored in Paris by Yves Saint Laurent, her personal couturier, and her hair given the full treatment by her travelling hairdressers. Her slim figure made its swaying, unsteady way along the windblown path, held up by two 'heavies'. She was followed by her best maid, Darlene, whose centre of gravity being in her rump, and her poundage considerable, was prevented from becoming what the Scripture calls 'a reed shaken by the wind'. She bounced along showing no signs of being any the worse for her recent use as a trampoline.

Magdalene's brother, Bubba, a ruddy faced young man, appeared dressed like Mel Gibson in "Braveheart"; feathered blue bonnet, targe, and claymore and all! It was Bubba's belief that William Wallace had not been put to death in London, but had, in fact, escaped to Virginia, changed his name to O'Hara to fool his pursuers, and founded a colony. This absurd notion had led him to appear ludicrously clad in a calf length Wallace tartan kilt held up by a belt with two holsters containing silver pistols. Had Archie not been struggling to stay on his feet, he would have ordered the said Bubba to disarm before worship commenced.

The crowd delivered a moderate cheer, which blew away off into the North Sea as soon as uttered. Tottering and swaying, Archie forcefully declined to lead the bride to the rocks where the Marquis awaited her holding down the table. Magdalene immediately saw Archie's point for she had no wish to be lifted off her feet and end up in Davy Jones's locker. The matter was settled when the second table gave up its resistance and took off out into the ocean.

The courtyard gave some, but not much shelter to anyone over four feet tall, the wall being only waist high, however it was better than nothing, and by gathering there the danger of drowning was removed. Another table was set up, with heavier rocks as ballast, and Archie took station behind it facing the clinging couple who, wanting an unconventional wedding, were certainly getting one in full.

Archie was about to perform his duties when recorded music came from somewhere and Bubba and Darlene began singing a nasal song from one of their sister's Grammy winning albums. In other circumstances, the effect on those present who appreciated that sort of thing might well have been pleasing, but with the wind making musical appreciation of minimal appeal to the hearers, the melody passed unnoticed; 'Gone With the Wind' so to speak.

Magdalene swayed about, fluttering and dancing in the breeze like one of William Wordsworth's daffodils. Feet set firmly apart, the Marquis looked like Napoleon in sombre mood after his defeat at Waterloo. The officiating Archie, staggering from side to side, took a very close look at the bride's face to be sure it really was Magdalene this time round, then opened with a prayer. This was rendered inaudible by the wind which lifted his B.D. degree hood and completely covered his face. After disentangling his physog, and restoring his vision, he announced the hymn, shouting it out in a muffled voice. This involved distributing hymn sheets, no easy task in the force four, which blew them away as soon as issued. The hymn was omitted by popular request of the ladies present who were

171

desperately trying not to forfeit their treasured fancy headgear.

After his recent experience of violent interruptions at weddings, Archie took the precaution of leaving out of the ceremony the words about "anyone...just 'cause why they may not be lawfully joined in marriage" and so forth. This time, no crazy Confederate cavalrymen appearing, and no objections being raised, vows were duly taken, rings exchanged, kisses offered and received. It was all over except for a few feeble attempts at throwing confetti and rice at the seagulls wheeling and screeching overhead. It was what you could call a 'low key' wedding, apart from the high key whistling of the wind tearing at the beach.

As they say in the windy cities of Edinburgh and Chicago: "It's an ill-wind that blows nobody any good." (in Glesga it 'blaws naebidy ony good'). So, as any school teacher cognisant of pupils' behaviour in class will tell you, high winds make for high spirits. After young Duke had taken the newly weds off in his polished B.M.W. (purchased on Magdalene's expense account), and driven them the five hundred yards from the harbour to the sanctuary of the Crown Hotel the guests followed after them struggling against the bellows of Typhoeus until safely reaching the much desired shelter of the wedding reception..

The ladies quickly disappeared inside each anxious to sort a distressingly wrecked hair-do, while the men besieged the bar gasping for breath and a dram. Everyone was soon restored to the aforementioned high spirits. Glasses in hand, greetings were exchanged, introductions pursued cheerfully. Archie was introduced to Veronica's mother, Grace, a tall, diamond studded lady who was exchanging best-of-friends telephone numbers and addresses with Sylvia as they sipped vodkas together in a cosy corner. A knot of film stars, sports personalities, and other *prominenti*, of whom Archie had only the sketchiest knowledge, were gathered around Margaret, the wife he had hardly seen all day. She was in tip top form judging by the hilarity. She's some woman, he grinned, and not for the first time since they met long ago, he took a notion to her again and thought - she's some woman!

It transpired that father of the bride Jim was Veronica's step-father; he was also a Senator for Maine, or was it Vermont? (a bit confusing, Archie had had a few by this time). Seems his great grandfather had found a goldmine in the California Gold rush of '49, used the proceeds to build railroads and skyscrapers and, after a lifetime of struggle and toil, had ended up with nothing to show for his labours but a huge fortune. This he had passed on to his heirs who appreciated his memory by endowing several museums and hospitals in his name. This was most gratifying to Archie, who, though never a materialist had several good works of his own which could benefit from the Yankee dollar.

While they were arranging a golf outing together, who should turn up but Veronica and Gordon, the anticipation of connubial bliss showing in their glowing faces. They were greeted with immense enthusiasm and joy, in a manner reminding Archie of the reception in Lystra of Paul and Barnabas who were taken to be the gods Zeus and Hermes.

"Where is V's mother?" asked Margaret when she circulated in her husband's direction.

"She is dead," said Archie sorrowfully, "but if you ask me, she is just using that as an excuse for not being here at her daughter's wedding."

For a split second Margaret was almost taken in - people never knew whether Archie was being serious or mischievous.

"That's NOT funny! V's mother was sitting with me in the church and, if you can be bothered to look, you'll see Grace is over there with my mother. I see Magdalene's Mum Doris has joined them. Grace is wearing a Stella McCartney dress - see, look."

"Magdalene's mother? Is she here as well?"

Before flouncing off, beaming from ear-ring to ear-ring, to enjoy the adoration of her Guild ladies, Margaret added a parting wifely shot: "For goodness sake Archie, tidy yourself up and comb your hair."

He obediently ran his fingers through his hair, and looked over to a corner table where Sylvia sat with the aforementioned two ladies, Grace and Doris, the two mothers' of the two brides, and a fourth lady...could it be? Yes, it was Cynthia. There they were 'The Golden Girls'; Grace, a high society lady from New England; Doris, an 'Annie Oakley' look-alike; a very cheerful Sylvia; and Her Ladyship hiding under a huge blue hat - the four of them in cahoots, getting on together splendidly from the look of things, though what they were laughing and talking about Archie could only guess. I knew Cynthia would turn up thought Archie with a wry smile which exuded a spirit of goodwill towards one and all.

He wandered over to where Jim Marshall was talking to Leroy about Republican Party politics. It turns out this Leroy guy is Magdalene's father. Here was another piece of essential information enabling Archie to put together a "Who's Who" of the various relatives and avoid putting his foot in it during his speech by using the wrong names at what had become a mixed up double wedding reception.

174

Needless to say, the meal was splendid, the cake seven storeys high (give or take a storey or two), and the speeches were great - especially Archie's long tried and tested oration which greatly amused everyone in the audience except his dear wife who had heard it several hundred times before. A ceilidh band set the reels jumping and, to add a touch of class the famous tenor Placebo da Bingo, flown in and hired at great cost, sang popular arias from Italian operas, and songs from the shows. These, with Latin gestures of affection and respect, he dedicated to Sylvia, the heroine of the day, presenting her with a whole florist's shop of flowers to rapturous applause. Magdalene's uncle Billy Joe diversified the entertainment by appearing costumed as Elvis Presley, and giving a reasonable imitation of the King in motion; while other relatives formed a barber shop quartet and gave harmonious voice to "Carry Me back to Old Virginy", "On the Blue Ridge Mountains of Virginia" and, by popular request, "West Virginia My Mountain Home". Highlights of that memorable evening were Magdalene herself singing, "Stand by Your Man"; and her regained husband giving voice in French to *"La Mer"*, a song which pleased Magdalene's family members because they took it to be about riding a horse. Archie stumbled his way through the foxtrots, but redeemed his performance by waltzing Margaret romantically through the last waltz.

The wind dropped and a great calm descended as the long daylight hours of the Northern summer turned from the gloaming into the velvet darkness of the wee small hours. The two happy couples set off in their various ways: Magdalene, now the Marchioness de Mortgage, accompanied her tipsy Gallic husband to Sutor House; Veronica and Gordon made for the airport hotel. Much waving and joking speeded their departure while Katie fondled Veronica's bouquet as she wished them goodbye and good luck. The younger guests, who had remained to the end, made off somewhat noisily through the streets to enjoy follow up parties. Silence gradually fell over old St. Regulus.

Cheerily but wearily, Archie and Margaret made their way back to the manse accompanied by Sylvia who fell asleep in the car beside an unusually quiet Arthur. Margaret put Sylvia to bed and then went for her bath.

Archie stood awhile for a last, lingering puff at a cigar and a look out of his study window. I'm the luckiest man in the world, he thought: a happy family, a job I love, and every day I enjoy a view which cannot be rivaled anywhere in the world for scenic beauty. He looked down upon the dark waters of the Firth with its parked oilrigs lit up like Christmas trees, and into the far distance where the mountains of the west were reluctantly parting from the last lingering traces of this amazing day. Overhead the countless stars filled the sky with the Glory of God.

He stubbed out the cigar, remembered with great satisfaction that he had his Monday golf with the Colonel still to come and, feeling worn out and ready for his kip, he closed the curtains. Catching his father alone on the stairs heading for a welcoming bed, Arthur asked hesitantly: "Dad, could I speak to you for a minute about something."

"Oh no, Arthur" said his long-suffering father, "not you and Katie, not another bleeding wedding!"

"She's not a spy or anything like that," responded son number two, a bit miffed.

"I wouldn't bet on it," Archie said half seriously.

Hearing Margaret calling him to join her between the sheets, Archie McTaggart, M.A., B.D., M.C., drew the meeting to a close by quoting Scripture: "Sufficient unto the day is the evil thereof; see you in the morning, son, see you in the morning."

Printed in the United Kingdom
by Lightning Source UK Ltd.
134227UK00001B/19-75/P